# DATE DUE

| 4/6/18 | | | |
|--------|--|--|--|
| | | | |
| | | | |
| | | | |
| | | | |
| | | | |
| | | | |
| | | | |
| | | | |
| | | | |
| | | | |
| | | | |
| | | | |
| | | | |
| | | | |
| | | | |
| | | | |
| | | | |
| | | | |

# Post Traumatic Stress Disorder

# DISEASES & DISORDERS

# Post Traumatic Stress Disorder

## Peggy Thomas

LUCENT BOOKS

*An imprint of Thomson Gale, a part of The Thomson Corporation*

THOMSON
™
GALE

Detroit • New York • San Francisco • New Haven, Conn. • Waterville, Maine • London

LIBRARY OF CONGRESS CATALOGING-IN-PUBLICATION DATA

Thomas, Peggy.
   Post traumatic stress disorder / by Peggy Thomas.
      p. cm. -- (Diseases and disorders)
   Includes bibliographical references and index.
   ISBN 978-1-4205-0002-8 (hardcover)
   1. Post-traumatic stress disorder--Juvenile literature. I. Title.
   RC552.P67T52 2008
   616.85'21--dc22

                                                                2007035904

ISBN-10: 1-4205-0002-3

Printed in the United States of America

# Table of Contents

Nashoba Regional High School
Media Center

# "The Most Difficult Puzzles Ever Devised"

**C**harles Best, one of the pioneers in the search for a cure for diabetes, once explained what it is about medical research that intrigued him so. "It's not just the gratification of knowing one is helping people," he confided, "although that probably is a more heroic and selfless motivation. Those feelings may enter in, but truly, what I find best is the feeling of going toe to toe with nature, of trying to solve the most difficult puzzles ever devised. The answers are there somewhere, those keys that will solve the puzzle and make the patient well. But how will those keys be found?"

Since the dawn of civilization, nothing has so puzzled people—and often frightened them, as well—as the onset of illness in a body or mind that had seemed healthy before. A seizure, the inability of a heart to pump, the sudden deterioration of muscle tone in a small child—being unable to reverse such conditions or even to understand why they occur was unspeakably frustrating to healers. Even before there were names for such conditions, even before they were understood at all, each was a reminder of how complex the human body was, and how vulnerable.

6

While our grappling with understanding diseases has been frustrating at times, it has also provided some of humankind's most heroic accomplishments. Alexander Fleming's accidental discovery in 1928 of a mold that could be turned into penicillin has resulted in the saving of untold millions of lives. The isolation of the enzyme insulin has reversed what was once a death sentence for anyone with diabetes. There have been great strides in combating conditions for which there is not yet a cure, too. Medicines can help AIDS patients live longer, diagnostic tools such as mammography and ultrasounds can help doctors find tumors while they are treatable, and laser surgery techniques have made the most intricate, minute operations routine.

This "toe-to-toe" competition with diseases and disorders is even more remarkable when seen in a historical continuum. An astonishing amount of progress has been made in a very short time. Just two hundred years ago, the existence of germs as a cause of some diseases was unknown. In fact, it was less than 150 years ago that a British surgeon named Joseph Lister had difficulty persuading his fellow doctors that washing their hands before delivering a baby might increase the chances of a healthy delivery (especially if they had just attended to a diseased patient)!

Each book in Lucent's Diseases and Disorders series explores a disease or disorder and the knowledge that has been accumulated (or discarded) by doctors through the years. Each book also examines the tools used for pinpointing a diagnosis, as well as the various means that are used to treat or cure a disease. Finally, new ideas are presented—techniques or medicines that may be on the horizon.

Frustration and disappointment are still part of medicine, for not every disease or condition can be cured or prevented. But the limitations of knowledge are being pushed outward constantly; the "most difficult puzzles ever devised" are finding challengers every day.

# Bad Memories

The lights dim in the Southern California movie theater and former Marine sergeant Eric Schrumpf, who served in the Iraq war, tenses. He scans the audience for anyone who may be a threat. A man who appears to be Middle Eastern sits in the same row. Eric hears the man jangling something metal and a memory is triggered. Eric lunges toward the man believing he is a suicide bomber. An object falls to the floor. It is nothing more than a can of soda.

But to Schrumpf the jangling that triggered the attack sounded just like the tick of the grenade that landed at his feet while he was serving with the 5th Marine Regiment in southern Iraq in 2003. The grenade failed to explode but those fateful moments continued to replay in his memory months later. He found himself overreacting to normal, everyday situations.

In the summer of 2000, in the front of a rural schoolhouse in upstate New York, children from Bosnia play kickball. The summer sun shines above them and they act as if they do not have a care in the world, laughing and joking until a sound in the distance startles them. It is a fertilizing machine being used in the cornfield on the other side of the road. Frightened, the children run for cover inside the school building. It has been months since they last heard that noise, but last time it was not a farmer's harmless piece of equipment. They heard that noise during the war in Bosnia as soldiers marched down the street outside their homes firing their machine guns.

Some children who have lived through traumatic events, like those who were caught in the middle of the war in Bosnia, have been diagnosed with Post Traumatic Stress Disorder.

Everyone gets stressed. Students may feel stress when they have too many homework assignments, or when they feel pressure about their grades, or when they argue with friends, parents, or siblings. The list of stressful situations is endless. What might be stressful for one person may not affect another. Stress is part of everyday life and the human body has ways of coping with it.

But what happens when a person experiences a life-threatening event or is exposed to prolonged life-threatening situations? What Eric Schrumpf experienced in Iraq was not normal. And the Bosnian children's daily life in a war zone was not ordinary. The mind-body system that deals with everyday stressful situations becomes overloaded during extraordinary events. The brain is not able to turn off the stress response. Horrific memories and experiences are involuntarily relived. Sounds, sights and smells can trigger extreme reactions.

These are classic symptoms of the only psychological disorder linked with an outside cause—Post Traumatic Stress Disorder (PTSD).

# CHAPTER ONE

# Wounds of War

In 1865, Erastus Holmes staggered out of the infamous Confederate POW camp in Andersonville, Georgia. He weighed no more than 85 pounds. Disease, starvation, and deprivation had reduced him to half the man he was as a quartermaster in the 5th Indiana Cavalry Regiment. But the end of the Civil War did not bring an end to his suffering. Holmes went home but could not stop thinking about the horrors he had witnessed. He obsessively built a model of the Andersonville Prison in his backyard, then spent 25 years in the Indiana Hospital for the Insane.

If Holmes were alive today, he might have been diagnosed with Post Traumatic Stress Disorder (PTSD), a disorder caused by experiencing a horrific tragedy resulting in nightmares, flashbacks, avoidance behavior, excitability and other symptoms. But during the Civil War, physicians called afflictions like his Soldier's Heart, or Irritable Heart. They did not yet understand the workings of the brain, and were just beginning to study mental illnesses. They thought that a disease of the heart caused emotional symptoms.

Dr. Jacob Mendez Da Costa, a physician during the Civil War, recorded how many wounded Union soldiers had rapid heart rates and high blood pressure combined with severe exhaustion and the ability to be easily startled.

No matter what the disorder was called, it was clear that many men who fought in the war suffered from their experiences. One study that looked at medical and pension records from the Civil War confirmed this, and suggested that the soldiers who witnessed the most death and destruction were more likely to suffer from anxiety, depression and other illnesses later in life. And the youngest soldiers, ages nine to seventeen, were almost twice as likely as soldiers over thirty years of age to show signs of mental illness after the war.

## Shell Shock

The same symptoms were seen in soldiers who fought in World War I. This time it was called Shell Shock or Combat Fatigue. The term Shell Shock gave the impression that the person had been close to an explosion, but military physicians realized that proximity had nothing to do with it. Charles Myers, a psychologist serving at the front, wrote that Shell Shock occurred "where the tolerable or controllable limits of horror, fear, anxiety etc. are overstepped."[1]

The battles were so intense that it was not uncommon to find soldiers on the battlefield suffering from amnesia, unable

Soldiers returning from serving in World War I experienced what is now called Post Traumatic Stress Disorder, but at the time the collection of symptoms was known as Shell Shock.

to recall their name or the name of their hometown. There was no room for unfit soldiers at the front. They were evacuated, hospitalized and often treated with electric shock therapy. Men who wandered away from the front on their own were branded deserters and set before a firing squad.

Even after the war ended, physicians were dealing with veterans who still suffered. Observing WWI veterans at a Red Cross medical hospital near Liverpool, England, Major R.G. Rows, a physician with the Royal Army Medical Corps noted:

> In some cases the physical expression of a special emotion, such as fear or terror, persists for a long time without much change. This condition is usually associated with an emotional state produced by the constant intrusion of the memory of some past incident.[2]

A psychologist with the Royal Army Medical Corps, Dr. Millais Culpin, witnessed one of his patients experiencing a flashback and wrote: "He seemed to be living his experience over again with more than hallucinatory vividness, ducking as shells came over or trembling as he took refuge from them."[3]

Few doctors wrote about what these veterans experienced, and friends and family of the soldiers rarely spoke of it. It was an embarrassment to a military that needed strong fearless soldiers, and was viewed as a sign of weakness. This disorder was soon forgotten until soldiers started coming home from yet another terrible war.

## World War II

World War II had its share of veterans who came home with nightmares and anxiety, but the sense of victory overshadowed their problems. The men stoically raised their families and built careers without mentioning the horrors that they saw. "Society didn't want to hear it," said Andrew Pomerantz, the chief of mental health services for the Veterans Administration in Vermont. "You don't want to hear that your hero who has just come back from winning the war is troubled by what he did over there and the people he bombed, the people he shot. People didn't want to hear that kind of thing."[4] But the emotions and memories that they buried inside would occasionally surface, days, months and years later.

Dr. Eugene Kaplan experienced this thirty years after the end of the war. He was cross-country skiing through the mountains of Vermont and the roar of a diesel engine and the rumble of tire treads triggered this response: "Suddenly I'm off the trail and on my belly calling for my bazooka team from the rear of my squad. The tank was coming closer and closer. I was sweating, my heart pounding, and my pulse racing."[5] For those few seconds Kaplan was transported back to his infantry unit ready to fire at a German tank until he fully realized his situation. It was not a tank. It was only a bulldozer in a nearby field.

## Post-Vietnam Syndrome

While most veterans from World War II suffered in silence, many of the veterans of the Vietnam War were activists. Even though soldiers had been tormented for centuries, the medical community still had not adequately recognized their symptoms as a defined and treatable illness. There was no medical name for the set of symptoms that plagued so many veterans, and no organization to help them. Some veterans repressed the bad memories deep inside to lead what they thought were normal lives, while others acted out, abusing alcohol and drugs.

In the early 1970s, a small group of veterans in New York City got together to talk about their feelings. They had never heard that intense stress could cause lasting effects, but they did know that something was wrong. "We were talking a mile a minute and jumping on each other's stories, and we suddenly realized we all had similar kinds of experiences and we were having the same kinds of problems,"[6] Vietnam veteran Jack Smith said in an interview on National Public Radio. The group decided to meet again and invited two psychiatrists to participate.

Dr. Jay Lifton and Dr. Chaim Shatan had read about "war neurosis," but after meeting with the group of Vietnam War veterans they had witnessed it in more than one person. In 1972 Chaim Shatan wrote an article about this phenomenon in the New York Times and called it Post-Vietnam Syndrome. It was the first time that this disorder had been so publicly acknowledged and examined. The article attracted the attention of hundreds of vets relieved to know that they were not alone, as well as the attention of the Veterans Administration that was uneasy about this new diagnosis of an old problem. The government was afraid that it would go bankrupt paying for treatment and benefits. But Shatan, Lifton and Smith did not let that concern them. Their only priority was to get help for soldiers. One way

After meeting with each other, many Vietnam veterans realized that they were suffering from the same set of symptoms, which came to be called Post-Vietnam Syndrome.

to do that was to get Post-Vietnam Syndrome recognized offi-
cially by the American Psychiatric Association.

## A New Disorder

A mental disease or disorder becomes an official part of the
medical vocabulary after much deliberation and debate by
members of the American Psychiatric Association (APA). Then
it is defined and listed in the APA's Diagnostic and Statistical
Manual (DSM), a thick text of all legitimate and recognized
mental illnesses.

The first edition (DSM-I) was written in 1952 and included
the first attempt to define this disorder that so many men from
WWII and wars past had suffered from. It was called Gross
Stress Reaction. But the name and definition of this disorder
seemed to be reinvented each time a new generation of doctors
tried to treat a new generation of soldiers. It even disappeared
from the second edition of the manual.

In the late 1970s a committee of psychiatrists examined the
research provided by Lifton and Shatan supporting the existence of Post-Vietnam Syndrome. They also studied data from
other trauma research that included rape victims, Holocaust
survivors and people who had survived natural disasters. The
evidence clearly showed that traumas other than war could
cause similar severe symptoms. Post-Vietnam Syndrome was
renamed Post Traumatic Stress Disorder (PTSD) to account
for these other influences, and was added to the third edition
(DSM-III) in 1980.

Defining and identifying the condition was important for two
reasons. First, it allowed veterans to get the help they needed.
In 1989, Congress mandated the Department of Veteran Affairs
to establish the National Center for PTSD. Secondly, it crushed
the notion held for decades that the symptoms of Post Traumatic Stress Disorder were caused by inherent weakness, or
character flaws.

Lance Corporal Blake Miller and his wife arrive at the Veterans Hospital for Miller's psychiatric evaluation. Miller was diagnosed with Post Traumatic Stress Disorder after serving in Iraq.

# The National Center for Post Traumatic Stress Disorder

Within the Department of Veterans Affairs, the National Center for PTSD (NCPTSD) is the government's arm for research and education of this disorder. It consists of seven academic centers around the country with its headquarters in White River Junction, Vermont. Over the past 15 years, NCPTSD has broadened their research to include all types of trauma, not just combat-related PTSD. Their goal is to quickly turn scientific research into useful clinical practice so that veterans and others get the best care.

## Post Traumatic Stress Disorder

Today Post Traumatic Stress Disorder is defined as an anxiety disorder that can occur after experiencing or witnessing a traumatic or life-threatening event that causes intense feelings of fear or helplessness. Although many situations can be traumatic, the disorder primarily arises from life-threatening incidences such as war, terrorism, rape, abuse, a severe accident, or natural disasters like hurricanes and tornados.

According to the National Center for PTSD, about 60 percent of men and 50 percent of women will experience a traumatic event in their lifetime. But only about 6 to 8 percent of the population will experience PTSD. That means that 5 to 6 million adult Americans suffer from the disorder. Researchers estimate that number will rise over the next decade because of increased exposure to the growing turmoil in the world.

PTSD is a complex disorder with several components. To be diagnosed, a patient must exhibit three types of symptoms: re-experiencing symptoms, avoidance behaviors, and symptoms of hypervigilance.

# Re-experiencing Symptoms

Re-experiencing symptoms include nightmares or upsetting memories of the trauma. Young children often repeat aspects of the trauma in their play, and adults may feel as if the event is about to re-occur. In severe cases patients have flashbacks that feel so real the person sees, smells, and hears the same sensations they experienced at the time of trauma. Reliving the event in such an intense way brings on a swell of emotions, overwhelming the person with the same fear and helplessness they felt during the traumatic event. During such flashbacks, the person is no longer aware of the real world, but mentally stuck in the moment of the tragic scene.

Some outside stimulus, like a sight, smell or sound that reminds the person of the past traumatic event, often triggers these flashbacks and bad memories. Vietnam vets frequently associated the smell of diesel fuel with flashbacks of combat and transport helicopters. Several weeks after the September 11 terrorist attack on the World Trade Center a brisk wind kicked up the odd smell of burned buildings and bodies. Many people reported feeling sick and panic stricken all over again. They left work and only felt safe again when they were off the Manhattan Island.

# Avoidance Behaviors

Avoidance behaviors appear as the person consciously or unconsciously tries to avoid experiencing any situation that reminds them of the traumatic event. For example, people who have narrowly survived fatal car crashes may refuse to drive or get into a car. A woman who has been raped in an alley may avoid dark narrow places.

PTSD sufferers may also avoid meeting individuals who remind them of the traumatic event. Michael Risenhoover, a police captain who responded to the Oklahoma City bombing stayed in his house for weeks after the bombing. In such a small town everyone had been affected by the disaster, and he could not bear to see his neighbors. Eventually he moved to California to distance himself from the scene of the crime.

Police Captain Michael Risenhoover, who was on the scene in the aftermath of the Oklahoma City bombing in 1995, stayed in his house for weeks after the bombing due to PTSD.

Risenhoover may also have been avoiding the emotions he would have felt by seeing others who had been affected by the bombing. Avoiding emotions is another behavior common with PTSD patients. They may feel numb to what happens in the outside world. Psychotherapist Belleruth Naparstek recalls that one of her patients who had been abused as a child retreated from her family and only kept in touch with them by voice mail. Many veterans suffering from PTSD divorce because they cannot reconnect with their spouses on an emotional level. They

# U.S. Veterans Still Suffer

World War II—The National Center for PTSD estimates that one in twenty WWII veterans may have suffered symptoms of PTSD, and in 2005, 25,000 WWII vets received disability compensation for PTSD-related symptoms.

Korean War—Although no comprehensive study has been conducted, it has been estimated that as many as 30 percent of U.S. soldiers who fought in Korea may have symptoms of PTSD. Almost 11,000 veterans received compensation in 2005.

Vietnam War—The original study conducted between 1986 and 1988 reported that 30 percent of Vietnam veterans showed signs of PTSD. But a revised report in 2006 puts that figure closer to 19 percent. In 2005, more than 179,000 veterans received disability compensation.

Gulf War—Studies vary, but between 3 and 8 percent of the 697,000 troops suffer symptoms of PTSD. 2005 records show that 19,000 were compensated.

Afghanistan and Iraq War—As of August 2007, the 73,000 veterans who have fought in Iraq and Afghanistan, nearly 34,000 have been diagnosed with PTSD.

feel they have no connection with the rest of the world; they have no future.

Amnesia is an extreme form of avoidance. The mind refuses to remember the traumatic event at all. Patients with PTSD typically show a combination of three or more types of avoidance behaviors.

## Hypervigilance Symptoms

Another facet of the diagnosis is showing at least two types of hypervigilance symptoms, which include feeling constantly alert and on edge. In a war situation hypervigilance assures a soldier's survival. If he lets his guard down, the enemy might kill him. But at home this feeling of constant alertness may manifest itself in insomnia, irritability, anger, trouble concentrating and a sharp startle reflex.

A staff sergeant home from Iraq admitted to driving down the highway military-style. He scanned the horizon, swerved around garbage and subconsciously kept a lookout for a white Chevy Suburban like the one that sprayed machine-gun fire at his squad back in Iraq. One day it happened. Two white SUVs appeared in his rearview mirror. The sergeant veered off the road. His heart was pounding. "Man," he said. "It's a good thing I don't carry a gun."[7]

## Lingering Effects

Nightmares, feeling on edge, and avoidance are natural coping mechanisms and occur in many survivors of trauma. But most people return to normal within a short time. People who suffer from PTSD experience these symptoms for a much longer period. "What we know about trauma and PTSD is that it runs a natural course," said Dr. John Bradley, chief of outpatient psy-

A Navy psychiatrist talking to one of his PTSD patients on the phone. According to some psychiatrists, people who experience PTSD symptoms for more than thirty days should seek help.

chiatry at Walter Reed Army Medical Center. "Most of its symptoms gradually resolve. A person who still has symptoms after 30 days needs to seek help."[8]

Another facet of the diagnosis is that symptoms adversely affect normal life. Anyone who has experienced a tragedy might take time off from work or want to be alone for a while. But this common reaction is magnified in people who suffer from PTSD. They find it difficult to function normally at work and in social situations for many months, or even years. They may have problems with their marriages or lose their jobs.

How does an outside event cause such havoc in a person's life? In the same way that a body is injured in a car crash, the brain can be physically changed by a traumatic experience. Although scientists are just beginning to understand how the brain works, they already have evidence of physical adverse effects of trauma.

# Everybody Gets Stressed

**A**n early human trudges through thick brush. His stomach growls as he searches for food. To his right, he hears the snarl of an animal and a tingle runs down his spine. His heart pounds, breathing becomes heavier and his muscles tense. He no longer feels hungry. He is ready for an attack because he remembers what that snarl means.

Thousands of years later, a businesswoman crosses the street intent on getting to her next appointment. A car screeches around the corner. Without thinking, she jumps back, breathless and shaking. The next time she approaches that intersection she will remember to look twice before crossing.

The same survival mechanism that helped ancient humans stay alive in a dangerous wilderness is what keeps people alive in hazardous situations today. It is called the fight-or-flight response and it starts in the brain. Although scientists are only just beginning to appreciate how complex the brain-body interactions are, they do know that just as the brain controls other body functions without a person realizing it, the brain also monitors and responds to stress automatically. So in order to understand the impact of a super-stressful event like combat, rape or murder, we first have to understand how the brain works and how it reacts to normal stress.

## The Alarm System in the Brain

The brain is not one single mass. It is made up of several different structures that interact with each other and have distinct functions. The area that deals with stress, called the limbic system, is found deep inside the brain and is considered one of the most primitive parts of the brain. It is essentially the same in all mammals, and it controls the most basic survival behaviors, producing responses that a person does not consciously control.

Nestled in this part of the brain are the thalamus, hippocampus, amygdala, and hypothalamus. These structures work together to determine what emotions are attached to what the ears, eyes and other sensory organs perceive. Is the person at the door dangerous or friendly? Is the bark of a dog threatening or welcoming?

This diagram shows the hippocampus, thalmus, and amygdala, all structures of the human brain that determine what emotions are attached to what the sensory organs perceive.

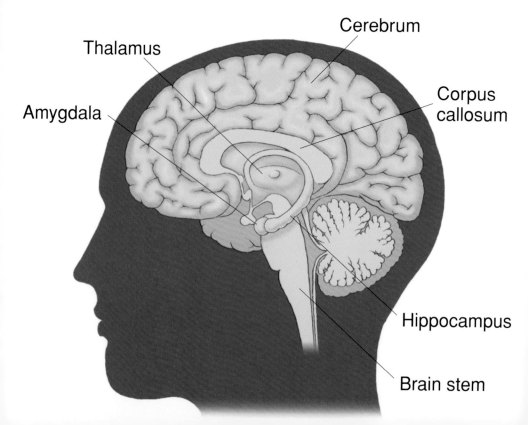

# The Neuron

The building blocks of the brain are cells called neurons. The neuron is made up of three parts: a cell body, a long section called the axon, and many shorter branches called dendrites. All communication happens through complex networks of neurons.

The space between neighboring neurons is called the synapse. Neurons communicate with each other using chemicals called neurotransmitters that are released from the ends of the axons and travel into the synapse. Then the neurotransmitters attach to special receptor sites on the neighboring cell and the message is transmitted. There are also special sites at the end of the axon that pull back excess chemicals. They are called reuptake sites and effectively stop a message once it has been received by the other neuron.

The thalamus lies in the center of the limbic system and serves as the gateway between the outside world and the inner brain. It is the central relay point where information from the senses comes in and is distributed to the appropriate parts of the brain. It screens information and determines what is and what is not important to react to.

The hippocampus is a sausage-shaped organ that puts data into context. It connects the information that the senses perceive with other information already in the brain. It organizes memories, retrieves memories when necessary, and sends memories out to the appropriate places in the cerebrum for long-term storage. It helps people have a sense of place and time—lets them know what is the past, present and future and how to relate new information to past information.

The amygdala is an almond-shaped structure about an inch long that is involved in learning and memory. It regulates emotions and connects them, especially fear and aggression, to a stimulus. Rats that have had their amygdales removed show no fear and calmly approach cats unaware of their danger.

The hypothalamus is only the size of pea but it directs a lot of important functions. It controls the chemical messengers that tell the body how to react to certain stimulus. It can make a person feel anger, sadness or happiness. It triggers the adrenaline rush one might experience during an accident or during a roller coaster ride. It also controls the primitive fight-or-flight response.

All of the structures are connected through a complex system of nerve cells. And according to psychiatry professor Ned Kalin, at the University of Wisconsin-Madison, "More and more we're beginning to believe, and the evidence is pointing to the idea, that it's the circuits that are important, not just the structure per se."[9]

## Chemical Messengers

Nerve cells communicate with each other and the rest of the body through chemical messengers called neurotransmitters and hormones. Neurotransmitters are chemicals released by nerve cells (also called neurons) to pass information from cell to cell. There are many neurotransmitters, and they act within the synapses, or spaces, between nerve cells. Hormones are chemicals released by glands like the adrenal gland or pituitary gland. Neurotransmitters travel a relatively small distance from one neighboring neuron to another, while hormones travel through the bloodstream throughout the body to reach the cells they target.

These chemical messengers are keys that fit into a target cell's lock. They may tell a cell to activate, or to stop work. For example, the neurotransmitter acetylcholine makes a cell more excitable, increasing its activity. GABA (gamma-aminobutyric acid), on the other hand, calms or inhibits a target cell. A healthy brain has a balance of inhibitory and excitatory chemicals.

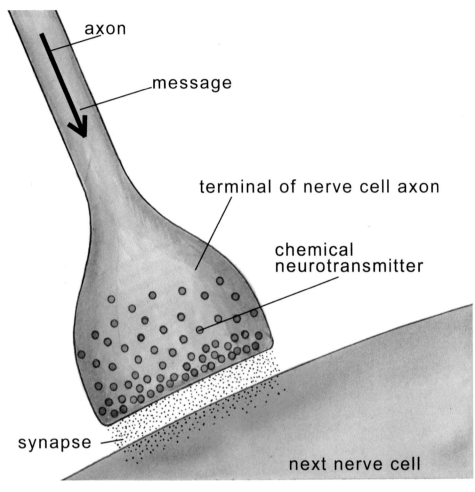

axon

message

terminal of nerve cell axon

chemical
neurotransmitter

synapse

next nerve cell

An illustration showing how the neurotransmitters are released by
the nerve cells, or neurons, and passed to the next neuron through
the synapse.

## Setting Off the Alarm

The brain is always taking in stimuli from what the eyes see,
what the ears hear, what the nose smells, and any other sensory
information. The data from the senses are sent to the thalamus,
which screens out unimportant information.

The important data is sent to the hippocampus which will determine what the information means. It could be the sound of a gunshot, movement in a dark alley, or the feeling of a snake slithering against the skin. The hippocampus asks: Have I experienced this sensation before? What did it mean in the past? What other sensory details are there? If the hippocampus perceives a threat to survival then the amygdala switches on the fear response and tells the hypothalamus to sound the alarm.

When activated, the hypothalamus releases CRF (corticotropin-releasing factor) that switches on two brain body connections—the sympathetic nervous system and the adrenal-cortical system—that will prepare the body to respond to the threat.

The sympathetic nervous system works on nerve pathways throughout the body to send messages. It sends out impulses to glands and muscles and tells the adrenal gland, located just above the kidneys, to pump out epinephrine, norepinephrine and other hormones into the bloodstream. Instantly the heart beats faster and the bronchial tubes open wider for easier breathing. The blood pressure rises to pump more oxygen-rich blood to the brain and to the muscles in the arms and legs.

# Brain Chemistry

Neurotransmitters come in two varieties: inhibitory and excitatory. In simple terms, inhibitory neurotransmitters like GABA and serotonin turn off or decrease the nerve impulses in the brain. Excitatory neurotransmitters like norepinephrine and epinephrine turn on or increase the nerve impulses. An imbalance in this delicate system can result in many of the symptoms seen in patients with PTSD. Too much norepinephrine results in a keen startle response, hypervigilance, flashbacks and nightmares. Too little serotonin causes depression, aggressive behavior, suicidal thoughts and anxiousness.

The pupils of the eyes dilate to let in as much light as possible and take in every visual detail. The other senses become keener and stress hormones enhance memory formation. That is why a person remembers even the tiniest details about a horrible event, as if it happened in slow motion.

At the same time, the CRF (corticotropin-releasing factor) switches on the pituitary gland, which pumps ACTH, or adrenocorticotropic hormone, into the bloodstream. It travels through the blood to activate the adrenal glands so that they release cortisol and other hormones. Cortisol keeps the initial burst of energy high, and keeps the blood pressure elevated for a longer period of time. Certain body functions like digestion, reproduction and the immune system that are not necessary during an emergency are temporarily shut down. At a moment's notice,

A Magnetic Resonance Imaging (MRI) in orange of the hypothalamus in the human brain. At any given time the hypothalamus can activate thirty different hormones that will get the body ready to fight or to flee a situation.

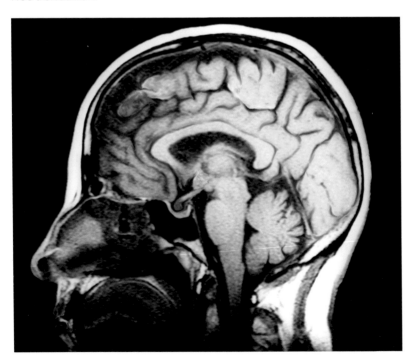

the hypothalamus can activate thirty different hormones that will get the body ready to fight or flee.

Once the threat is gone, the brain releases a different set of chemical messengers to halt the stress response bringing the body back to a normal resting state. Whatever was activated, accelerated or increased is deactivated, decelerated and decreased.

## Too Much Stress

Although the stress response is life-saving in the short term, it can be damaging to the body if activated for too long. Those who suffer from PTSD have lived through an event so powerful that it actually changes the chemistry of the brain, causing symptoms like constant alertness, nightmares, sleeplessness, depression or flashbacks. These symptoms occur when the normal healthy balance of brain chemicals tips out of balance.

During a PTSD-influencing event, the amygdala goes into hyperdrive and the hippocampus is unable to rein it in. Too much CRF floods the system, and the body cannot shut off the fight-or-flight response. Patients with PTSD have elevated levels of norepinephrine coursing through their system, giving them a sense of hypervigilance, a hair-trigger startle response, intrusive memories, and flashbacks. They also exhibit abnormally low levels of serotonin. Serotonin is a neurotransmitter that influences mood and may fuel the fear response. Low levels of serotonin can make people feel depressed, numb, emotionally flat, and may cause them to have a poor memory.

Scientists are still figuring out how each chemical imbalance affects the brain, but they do know that it is a physical injury as real as a cut on the skin. For example, research has shown that the hippocampus, which is vital for memory and learning, shrinks in size. Scientists experimenting with rats showed that daily injections of cortisol for several weeks killed brain cells in the hippocampus. The same results occurred without the injections, when rats were put under stress for a specified amount of time each day.

Dr. J. Douglas Bremner, the director of Mental Health Research at the Atlanta Veterans Administration Medical Center, studied the brain scans of Vietnam veterans.

> What we found is that the hippocampus was smaller in the PTSD patients than the comparison group, 8% smaller for the right hippocampus. We also found that the more problems the veterans had with memory, the smaller the hippocampus.[10]

The toxic level of cortisol caused the neurons to become overstimulated. They literally died of excitement. This cell death correlated with the veterans' symptoms of not being able to remember new information, and not being able to control the fear response that went along with the old memories. Other PTSD patients, including victims of child abuse and women who suffered non-combat trauma like rape, also have a hippocampus that is smaller than normal.

## Making Memories

The same parts of the brain that help a person escape from danger also play important roles in creating memories. That makes sense because when a person is attacked by a grizzly bear, it would be a good idea to remember the connection between the bear and danger so that the next time the person encountered a grizzly they could act swiftly.

There are several theories about how memories are created. There are basically three types of memory: short term or working memory, long-term or declarative memory, and procedural memory.

Procedural memory is used for skills that have been learned by repetition. For example, riding a bike, brushing teeth, getting dressed, and playing the piano all use this type of memory.

Like the RAM of a computer, short-term memory is used for everyday operations like following directions, adding numbers in your head or writing a sentence. The information is stored

Riding a bike is an example of a skill that is learned by repetition and makes use of procedural memory.

for a short time and then recycled. It does not become a permanent memory.

Long-term or declarative memory is the hard drive of the brain. In it is stored all the facts, names and information that you have ever learned. All of this information has to be processed through the hippocampus before it is consolidated and filed away in another part of the brain.

Fred Helmstetter at the University of Wisconsin showed how memories are stored in certain neurons. The brain is constantly forming and breaking neural connections. When a person learns something new, they are creating new pathways in their brain, new connections, and these are strengthened each time that memory is recalled. Every time a person remembers something, the memory is brought out of long-term memory into short-term memory for temporary use. In short-term memory, the memory can be altered. So each time a memory is remembered and restored it is subtly altered and goes back into the brain like a new version of a text document, rewritten and saved over an old one. So when a person recalls a memory, he is not only recalling the original memory but he is also recalling the last time he remembered it, and all the times before.

The center of memory organization is the hippocampus, and many studies have shown a correlation between the size of the hippocampus and the ability to remember well. One study showed that birds that store food and have to remember where they stored it have a larger hippocampus than birds that do not store food. And a study conducted among London taxi drivers showed that they too had a larger than normal hippocampus. This stands to reason, since taxi drivers must remember how to navigate through hundreds of busy city streets.

## Stressful Memories

The strongest memories usually have a strong emotional component. People tend to remember their proudest and happiest moments as vividly as their most frightening or embarrassing experiences. And many of those moments are linked to the

An illustration showing the amygdala and the hippocampus. In normal situations the amygdala and the hippocampus are able to work together to control stress reponses, however in PTSD the hippocampus is unable to rein in the fear response.

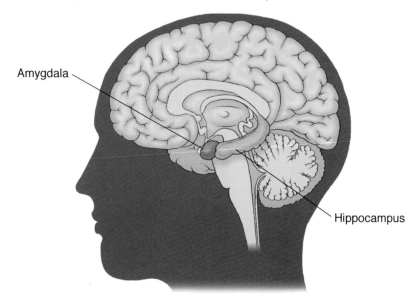

Amygdala

Hippocampus

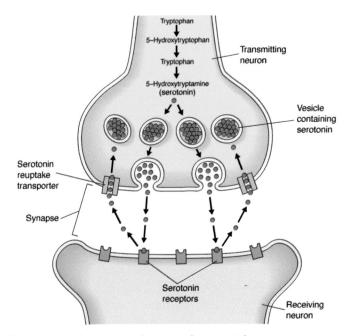

Tryptophan
↓
5–Hydroxytryptophan
↓
Tryptophan                          Transmitting
↓                                   neuron
5–Hydroxytryptamine
(serotonin)

Vesicle
containing
serotonin

Serotonin
reuptake
transporter

Synapse

Serotonin
receptors
                                    Receiving
                                    neuron

An illustration of a neuron showing the special receptor sites on the neighboring neuron that delivers the message and the reuptake sites that stops the message once it is delivered.

stress response. The brain's chemistry is what links emotions to memories. Christa McIntyre, a researcher from UCI, said:

> Emotionally neutral events generally are not stored as long-term memories. On the other hand, emotionally grounding events, such as those on September 11, tend to be well-remembered after a single experience because they activate the amygdala.[11]

During a stress response, the stress hormones tell the amygdala and hippocampus that any memories recorded in the next few minutes need to be strong and vivid. The hippocampus usually acts to counterbalance the amygdala and the emotion associated with the memory, keeping it in context. So in normal situations, emotion can help us remember things, but extremely emotional and stressful events can damage that process.

In PTSD the stress is so severe or continual that the flood of chemicals sears the memory into the brain, and the hippocampus is unable to rein in the fear response associated with it. Every time a person recalls the trauma, the exceptionally vivid memory transfers back to the hippocampus, where it triggers the release of more hormones. The person experiences a flashback. The pulse rises, the breathing quickens, and the person recalls smells and sounds as if it were happening at that moment. This vicious cycle is reinforced each time the memory is recalled.

Some PTSD patients often find it hard to remember other things. In this case, there may have been too much cortisol that prevents the brain from laying down a new memory or from accessing an existing one. A 1999 study showed that four days of high levels of cortisol impaired the patient's ability to perform in a memory test. The test subjects felt they could not think straight.

However an animal study showed that cortisol affects memory only for a short period of time. Rats were stressed using electric shock and then made to go through a familiar maze. The rats had no problem when the shock was given two minutes before going through the maze, or when it was given four hours afterward. But when the shock was given 30 minutes before, the rats were unable to remember their way through the maze. Memory was not lost, but it was made temporarily inaccessible.

## The Impact of Stress

Not everyone who experiences a life-threatening tragedy will suffer harmful surges of brain chemicals or shrinkage of their hippocampus. Some people are more at risk than others to experience PTSD, and certain types of trauma are more likely to cause PTSD symptoms than others.

## CHAPTER THREE

# Society Under Stress

**O**n April 16 2007, a gunman killed 30 students and two professors on the campus of Virginia Tech. Dozens more were injured and everyone on campus felt a cauldron of emotions bubble up as they barricaded themselves in their dorms and watched the news unfold on the Internet. Hours later, students roamed the campus consoling one another and reassuring family members that they were all right. This event reminded the world how quickly life can change, and how a single horrifying act can have a lasting impact reaching beyond the boundaries of the immediately affected area.

In the months and years following the shooting doctors anticipate that more women than men on the campus will develop PTSD, and that those who stood closest to the gunman or were injured will be more deeply affected than those who were on the other side of the campus at the time of the shooting.

Although PTSD is a fairly recent addition to the diagnostic repertoire enough studies have been done worldwide to allow researchers to build a foundation of facts about who may be more vulnerable to the disorder and what kinds of trauma can trigger it.

## Gender and Age

According to a 2006 report by the National Institute of Mental Health, 7.7 million adults suffer from PTSD. Of that population, twice as many women than men are afflicted. This is consistent

Doctors anticipate that those injured during the Virginia Tech shooting, as well as those who stood closest to the gunman and women, will be more likely to develop PTSD in the future.

with studies conducted all over the world. Research in China, Nicaragua, Canada, France, Spain, Holland and Great Britain among others point to a strong gender difference in who is vulnerable to PTSD. It is unknown why this difference exists, but some psychologists speculate that in cases of assault, women are more often unwilling victims of violence, where as men may be more active participants. Women typically are also smaller than their assailants and may feel a greater sense of helplessness.

A person's age affects their susceptibility also. A child is more likely than an adult to develop PTSD. Scientists suggest that a child may not have the capacity to deal with the high levels of stress because their brains are not yet fully formed. They also have not developed behavioral coping skills to handle a life-threatening trauma. Those skills are learned through the process of dealing with age-appropriate stresses, and from watching parents and other adults.

## Social Factors

There are several other factors that appear to elevate a person's risk for PTSD. Previous psychological problems like depression or phobias make it more likely that a person will develop PTSD if they were to encounter a triggering event. Trauma early in life may also increase the risk. A child who is traumatized may not develop the normal ability to cope with stress leaving them more vulnerable. According to Chris R. Brewin, a professor of clinical psychology at the University of London, "This may produce an adult whose responses to new traumas are more extreme, are possibly more alarming in their own right and may take longer to extinguish themselves."[12]

Additional life stress, like marital problems, an illness or death in the family, just before or just after the triggering event adds to the equation. It may act as the last straw that pushes a person over the edge.

Although researchers are not sure of the link, it appears that a limited education is another risk factor. One study compared children with an average IQ of 115 or higher and found that they were less likely to develop PTSD by about twenty percent if exposed to a traumatic experience. Children with IQs below 115 had no advantage. Bruce Perry, a trauma expert, suggests

## At-Risk Children with Post Traumatic Stress Disorder

| Traumatic Event | Percentage of Children Who Develop PTSD |
|---|---|
| Witness to parental homicide or sexual assault | 100% |
| Sexually abused children | 90% |
| Witness to a school shooting | 70% |
| Exposure to community violence | 35% |

United States Department of Veterans Affairs. Available online at: http://www.ncptsd.va.gov/ncmain/ncdocs/fact_shts/fs_children.html

# First-responders

Police officers, firefighters, and emergency medical technicians see, hear and experience life-threatening traumas every day they go to work. They run into fires, haul bleeding bodies out of crushed cars and try to bring the dying back to life. Most can handle these difficult and emotional tasks because they rely on their professional training and skill to keep them focused. But suppressing or compartmentalizing one's emotions can be costly. Studies suggest that firefighters suffer from PTSD at a rate of 16 to 24 percent. That is more than double the rate of the normal population.

Although trained to deal with traumatic events on a daily basis, firefighters suffer from PTSD at a rate that is more than double of the normal population.

that more education may lead to more developed brain function and a greater ability to handle the added stress. A limited education, on the other hand, may leave the brain less able to cope.

People who lack a strong social network are also at risk. Talking to others and being supported by family and friends are important elements in coping with any trauma. Without that social support, recovery is less likely.

These risk factors are simply indicators or red flags that can identify who may need help after a traumatic event. But the key ingredient in developing PTSD is a triggering event that sets off the debilitating cluster of symptoms.

## Triggering Events

The DSM-IV describes a triggering event as one that "involves actual or threatened death or serious injury, or other threat to one's physical integrity...or a threat to the physical integrity of another person." It also involves a response of, "intense fear, helplessness, or horror."[13]

News coverage gives the impression that PTSD only develops after a massive event involving dozens of victims. War, terrorism, and natural disasters are powerful and PTSD-provoking traumas, but the triggering event can also be as individual and personal as a rape, a car accident, or child abuse.

## Child Abuse

The physical and emotional wounds of child abuse are deep and often life-threatening. The feelings of fear and helplessness are intense and can last into adulthood. An adult PTSD patient recounts the daily agony experienced many years after being abused as a child:

> For several years I was terrified of going to the dentist, the car wash, or anywhere that was confining." The patient had to sit in an aisle seat at the movies or on a plane and had a fear of any kind of authority figure. "I was even terrified to go to parent-teacher conferences for my children but made myself do it anyway...Nobody ever knew how much work it was to just not stay home and hide![14]

Many adults who have suffered abuse struggle to maintain an outwardly ordinary life, and try to avoid reminders of the past. They feel worthless, fearful, guilty, abandoned, isolated, and terrorized all at the same time. These are the same emotions that plague the young abused child.

Unfortunately, it is difficult to identify children who have been abused when there are no outward physical signs. A child's behavior is key to uncovering abuse. If a child shows signs of suffering PTSD and has not experienced an obvious triggering event, child abuse may be the cause. Children suffering from PTSD due to child abuse often act agitated or withdrawn; they

Many child abuse victims often suffer PTSD as adults as they recount the agony they experienced in their younger years.

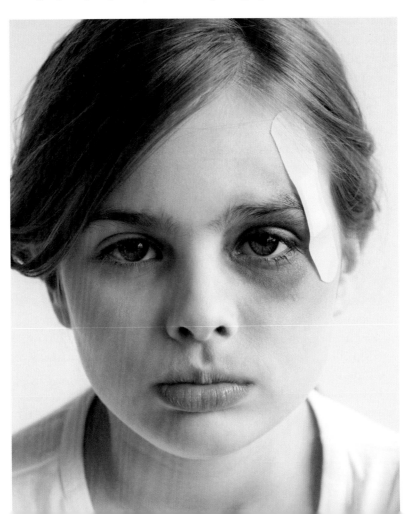

have frequent nightmares, and play in a repetitive manner often reenacting aspects of the abuse.

## Rape

According to the National Center for Victims of Crime, one-third of all rape survivors develop Post Traumatic Stress Disorder sometime in their lives. A week after a rape more than 90 percent will exhibit some of the PTSD symptoms, and 47 percent will continue to show signs after three months.

Rape is not only an attack on the body, but also an assault on a person's mind. Long after the body heals, a rape victim is left feeling betrayed, guilty, and shamed. Victims of rape are more likely to experience PTSD if they know their attacker, have a low sense of self worth, experience a negative response from family, or dissociate during the attack, which means they mentally distance themselves from what is happening to them physically.

Rape victims with PTSD symptoms commonly suffer from uncontrollable thoughts about the attack, nightmares, and flashbacks. They tend to withdraw from social situations, and they become almost numb and uninterested in living. Survivors also become hypervigilant, concerned with every strange sound or movement, and have difficulty sleeping.

## Car Accidents

"Serious car accidents are perhaps the most commonly experienced traumatic events in the United States," says Gayle Beck, a professor of psychology at the University of Buffalo. "The lives of accident survivors can be totally derailed by PTSD."[15] It is not uncommon for a survivor to avoid driving, be obsessed with thoughts of the accident and become estranged from family and friends because they will no longer drive. Some people find it difficult to concentrate and become irritable and develop insomnia.

PTSD is often overlooked because the emotional impact of car accidents is frequently underplayed by society, but nearly

Those people most likely to develop PTSD are those closest to the traumatic event, such as this man staring up at the smoking World Trade Center towers in New York City during the September 11, 2001, terrorist attacks.

nine percent of the 3.5 million people injured in accidents will develop the disorder.

## Terrorism

Before September 11, 2001, very few Americans worried about a terrorist attack affecting their lives. Now, polls indicate that about half of all U.S. citizens think about the possibility, occasionally or often. Organized terrorist attacks and brutal acts of mass violence like the shootings at Columbine High School or Virginia Tech have become a part of everyone's lives because they have become communal experiences shared through television, the Internet and print coverage.

But those most affected are the people closest to the center of the action. Eight months after the attack on the World Trade Center September 11, 2001, more than seven percent of the high school students living in the Bronx met the criteria for PTSD. Seven percent may not seem significant, however only two percent of students living in other areas showed symptoms of PTSD. Proximity to the event also had an effect among workers at the Pentagon on September 11 who reported symptoms of PTSD. Of those who worked on the day of the attack, twenty-two percent suffered those symptoms compared to only six percent who were not working that day. Those who were injured exhibited symptoms at a rate of forty-seven percent verses only ten percent of those who were unharmed.

## Natural Disasters

Natural disasters like tornados, earthquakes, tsunamis, or hurricanes have a devastating effect on entire communities. The devastation of Hurricane Katrina that hit the Gulf coast in 2005 covered 90,000 square miles of territory and destroyed social networks throughout the area that were designed to help people—churches, synagogues, mosques, schools, hospitals and community centers were wiped out. People were forced to move to new towns, where isolation from friends, family, and hometowns made PTSD symptoms worse.

# Growing Up After Hurricane Katrina

They lived in government-issued trailers lined up in fields like a refugee camp, or in the front yards of their demolished home. Others roomed in local hotels, or were forced to move to cities far from everything they knew. Of the children displaced by Hurricane Katrina, as many as 35,000, or one-third, suffer from PTSD. They constantly worry about the future, have nightmares, repeatedly talk about the hurricane, or avoid the topic altogether.

The Howard family fled to the roof of their New Orleans apartment when floodwaters rose. They huddled there for three days before being rescued by helicopter. They were lucky enough to move to Cleveland and start a new life, but the storm lingered in their children's behavior. Their nine-year-old daughter would not talk about it, and their five-year-old son could not sleep and clung to his mother.

According to psychologist Catherine Cottone, "The younger children are, the more their reaction depends on the adjustment of their parents and those around them." Unfortunately, the adults in the region suffer from PTSD at a rate ten times higher than the national average.

"Stressed-Out Victims of Katrina," *USA Today Magazine*, Vol 134, Oct. 2005, p 7.

Even those who did not move out of the area were constantly reminded of the disaster. Gina Barbe, a New Orleans resident, told a *New York Times* reporter, "I thought I could weather the storm, and I did—it's the aftermath that's killing me. When I'm driving through the city, I have to pull to the side of the street and sob."[16]

A home damaged by Hurricane Katrina. Many who were forced to move due to the storm suffered worse PTSD than those people who did not have to move.

According to Matthew Friedman of the National Center for PTSD, "Social support is the best way to prevent trauma after a disaster."[17] But he cautions that a full recovery takes time. In a comparison of two communities, one affected by flood and one untouched, the flood-damaged community had significantly higher rates of mental illness even 14 years later.

## Growing Up in a War Zone

The same long-term effect of PTSD occurs in people, especially children, who live in a war zone. Kareem was a happy child who loved to help his father work on cars in a garage in their war-torn village in Chechnya. One day, a mortar round came through the roof, exploding and killing Kareem's father instantly. Rescue workers thought Kareem was dead also, because he was covered in so much blood. Although he survived the explosion, Kareem did not bounce back quickly. For months he suffered from PTSD. He stopped talking and simply walked through life like a ghost. A summer trip to the United States a year later, slowly brought him out of his silent world before he returned home.

Kareem was lucky to have the help of an organization called Project Life that helps orphans recover from the stress of living in a war zone. Most children do not have such luxuries. Growing up with a battle raging around them is a chronic stress that desensitizes the person. They become numb to death and loss, and suffer nightmares. Without treatment, they may carry symptoms of PTSD for the rest of their life.

## Social Costs

Post Traumatic Stress Disorder not only affects individuals, but society at large. It has raised legal issues in a court of law, broken up marriages, and led to drug abuse and criminal activity.

Substance abuse is a common companion of PTSD. According to the Veterans Administration, 52 percent of people diagnosed with lifetime PTSD were also diagnosed with alcohol abuse or dependence. The number of PTSD patients who used illegal drugs was nearly three times that of the non-PTSD population.

Many veterans and survivors of trauma use alcohol and drugs to ease their psychological pain and distance themselves from bad memories. Although drugs and alcohol appear to lessen the severity of symptoms for a while, in the long term they often make the situation worse. Excessive alcohol and drug use prevents a person from working through the trauma and its aftermath. It adds to social isolation, driving a wedge between the person and their support system of friends and family. It causes depression, irritability, anger, and it can aggravate those who are already on constant alert. Overall, substance abuse decreases the effectiveness of medical and psychiatric treatments, and makes it less likely that a patient will seek treatment.

## Divorce

People who suffer from PTSD frequently respond to the trauma by withdrawing from life and from the people closest to them, even their spouses. PTSD sufferers feel they can't talk about their experience or share their feelings. Some lash out verbally, and sometimes they become physically aggressive. These behaviors make it difficult for friends and family to provide the support that a PTSD patient requires, and cause spouses to feel they have lost their connection to their partners.

According to the National Center for PTSD, rates of divorce for veterans with PTSD are two times greater than for veterans without PTSD. Moreover, veterans with PTSD were three times more likely than veterans without PTSD to divorce more than once.

## The PTSD Defense

PTSD also affects society at large in courts of law. According to the National Center for PTSD, "Almost half of all male Vietnam [war] veterans currently suffering from PTSD had been arrested or in jail at least once. Thirty-four percent more than once, and 11.5 percent had been convicted of a felony."[18] Because of the unusually high rate of crime associated with veterans suffering from PTSD it has been used successfully as a legal defense strategy and has affected state laws.

California lawmakers passed a bill that allowed judges to use their discretion when sentencing a veteran who had been diagnosed with PTSD. Instead of a prolonged jail time, the offender might be sentenced to probation and mandatory medical treatment.

Unfortunately, not all attorneys or expert witnesses use the defense properly. Often defense experts will over-diagnose the disorder, while experts for the plaintiff will downplay its effects on a person's behavior. According to Brandon Bolling, a military defense attorney and marine captain, "The PTSD issues help you make the guy a less serious offender. They reduce the punishment."[19] That is what happened for Matthew Denni, who returned from Iraq and killed his wife. When she announced she

World War II veteran Richard Keech was sentenced to 35 years to life in prison for killing his son-in-law. Keech said that his PTSD was the cause of the crime.

was leaving him for another man, Denni reached into a drawer, pulled out a handgun, and shot her in the neck. When the jury heard that Denni had a severe case of PTSD, they reduced his prison time by several years.

Post Traumatic Stress may be a psychiatric disorder, but its effects reach beyond the mind and emotions of sufferers. It is important to treat the disorder effectively, not only for the good of the individual, but also to benefit families and society.

# CHAPTER FOUR

# Treating PTSD

For many years, the most common treatment for PTSD was psychological debriefing. It usually consisted of a single session that took less than three hours and occurred within three days of the trauma. Patients were encouraged to talk about their feelings surrounding the event. It was thought that once patients had the opportunity to discuss their experiences, they could go on to live a normal life. Although this was a popular treatment, Dr. Matthew Friedman of the National Center for PTSD, admitted that studies showed no evidence that it reduced PTSD symptoms.

Today, creating a treatment plan for a patient with PTSD is like putting together a puzzle with many pieces. It is individualized for each person and the symptoms that they exhibit. The foundation of the plan usually involves standard psychoanalytical therapy or talk therapy, accompanied by medication if necessary. But over the last twenty years several other therapies have proven effective, especially cognitive-behavioral therapy (CBT), a form of talk therapy combined with behavior modification such as guided imagery, exposure therapy, and eye movement desensitization and reprocessing (EMDR).

## Cognitive-Behavioral Therapy

Talk therapy is based on the principle that thoughts and feelings are connected and that it is beneficial to get them out into the open. It looks at the way a person processed the event in

their minds at the time it occurred, and how they understand it afterwards. Talk therapy helps a person identify any troublesome thinking patterns.

Cognitive-behavioral therapy goes one step further. It identifies negative thoughts and emotions, teaches survivors a different way to think about the events, and helps them react in a more positive manner. Psychologists call this restructuring or reframing.

For example, a survivor of a natural disaster may feel guilt for having survived when others died. She may feel as if she could have done something more to help others. After talking the event over in cognitive-behavioral therapy sessions, she would be able to challenge her feelings and restructure the guilt into more healthy feelings of gratitude and pride for doing what she needed to do to survive.

Talk therapy gives patients much needed support and encouragement, and according to Lisa Najavits, of the National Center

This former Iraq War veteran (left) has been diagnosed with PTSD and is using talk therapy as a way to treat his symptoms.

# Therapy for All?

After a school shooting or a disaster at a factory, administrators may call in counselors from a commercial debriefing service. Such services promote the idea that a school or business might be negligent and could be sued if they do not offer counseling to all of their students or employees. But there is a debate on the effectiveness of giving therapy to everyone instead of targeting those who are most at risk of developing PTSD.

Some psychologists believe that using a blanket approach to therapy will catch vulnerable people who might have otherwise fallen through the cracks. Early screening is the only way to identify those that would benefit from cognitive-behavioral therapy, which is most effective if used soon after the event.

Others claim that early counseling can reinforce the event in people's memory when, for some, forgetting would be healthier. Critics of the blanket approach also suggest that, by making people focus on symptoms, counseling might encourage issues to emerge and persist when they might have dissipated over time.

This debate will most likely continue until a definitive study can be done, but until then, those responsible for the health of others will probably err on the side of offering therapy for all.

for PTSD in Boston, "It helps to know you're not crazy. People need to be told not to lie in bed all day and not to drink or use drugs to escape the emotional pain."[20] The best therapy gives the patient confidence in his or her ability to cope.

## Group Therapy

Sometimes meeting with others who have experienced the same type of trauma may help patients share their feelings. Group therapy offers a safe atmosphere for survivors to tell their stories: what psychologists call a "trauma narrative." Rape victims in particular recover faster with help from a support group, where they learn to come to terms with the past and alleviate stress in the present.

Gayle Beck, at the Center for Anxiety Research at the University of Buffalo works with PTSD survivors of traumatic car accidents. "Our recent work has shown that you can treat PTSD within a group therapy setting and obtain results that are just as effective as individual format CBT,"[21] Beck says. It is especially important given the rising cost of mental health services.

## Guided Imagery

For some people, talking about the event or their feelings can be difficult. They struggle to find the words to express themselves. Psychoanalyst Belleruth Naparastek explains that trauma often produces changes in the brain that impedes a person's ability to think and talk about the event, because the trauma was experienced both visually and through the other senses. If the verbal side of the brain is hindered, she suggests that it is more effective to use the visual side as a basis for treatment. "Imagery-based solutions use the right hemisphere of the brain—perception, sensation, emotion and movement—rather than the left side's standard cognitive functions of thinking, analyzing, verbalizing and synthesizing."[22]

Based on the principle that people can imagine themselves anywhere—under a cozy blanket, on top of a peaceful mountain, or on a quiet beach—guided imagery lets the imagination provide relief. It has also been called purposeful or directed daydreaming because it uses words and phrases "designed to evoke rich, multisensory fantasy and memory in order to create a deeply immersive, receptive mind-state that is ideal for catalyzing desired changes in mind, body, psyche, and spirit."[23]

Studies have shown that guided imagery does have an effect on the body. It can lower blood pressure, decrease the length of hospital stays and reduce pain in those who practice it. And for PTSD patients, it can relieve fears and increase coping skills. Researchers believe that it works primarily through the right hemisphere of the brain where the message is sensed, perceived, and felt, rather than being analyzed by the logical left side of the brain. Naparastek describes it like this:

> Imagery... sends its healing messages straight into the center of the whole person, where it can affect unconscious assumptions and jostle defeating self-concepts, while floating soft, appealing reminders of health, strength, meaning and hope.[24]

Some patients are directed to visualize themselves in a calming place so that each time an intrusive flashback occurs they

A woman working with a therapist on guided imagery, a form of treatment that will help PTSD patients increase coping skills and relieve fears.

can call up this vision. Adults who have suffered abuse may be guided back to the past where they can imagine themselves as an adult confronting the abuser or rescuing themselves as a child.

## Exposure Therapy

Exposure therapy literally exposes a survivor to aspects of the trauma so they can re-experience the feelings and fears that have overwhelmed them. In the safe surroundings of a therapist's office patients can face their fears and gain control of their emotions so that the trauma is no longer so stressful.

Patients are carefully and repeatedly exposed to the event in one of several ways. They may tell their story orally; alternatively, they might listen to someone else recite the events in the order they unfolded, or they might be shown detailed images. The exposure progresses slowly from least stressful to more traumatic. For example, a survivor of a boating accident

# How to Help a Person with PTSD

There are many ways to help a person who has been diagnosed with PTSD. According to the National Center for Post Traumatic Stress Disorder:

1. Learn all you can about PTSD and how it may affect a family member or friend.
2. Be a willing listener. Let them talk when they need to.
3. Encourage the person to seek professional help.
4. Encourage contact with friends and family. They may not know how to reach out.
5. Give them space if they need it. They may need time alone to think.
6. Be positive. Know that this is probably a temporary situation.

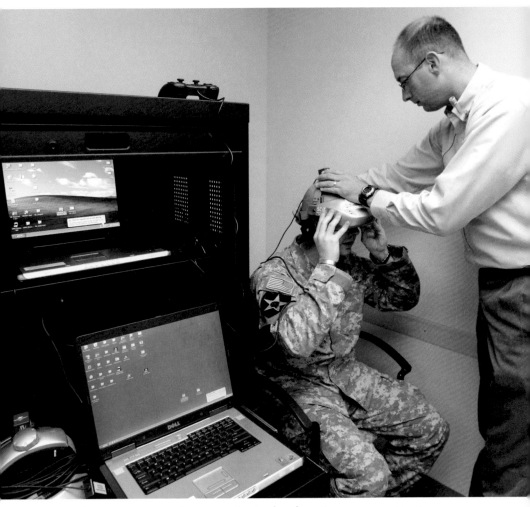

Treatment providers are using technology to expose patients to the event that triggered the PTSD. This form of treatment is called exposure therapy.

may be asked to tell what happened on that day. Imagine the details. The therapist will ask questions building the intensity of the exposure. How did it feel when the boat listed to one side? What did the water feel like as it rushed over your feet? In this way, the mind is desensitized by the repetition, and gradually the images and thoughts are no longer as frightening as they once were.

For more intensive exposure, therapists may take the patient to the scene of the trauma. For example, the survivor of the boating accident might be taken for a walk along the shoreline and eventually put on board a similar boat.

More and more, therapists are taking advantage of the technology to recreate stressful moments without leaving the safety of their offices. At New York Presbyterian Hospital's Weill Cornell Medical Center, patients put on headgear so they can hear sound recordings from the September 11 attack on the World Trade Center and watch images of buildings collapse as they appear on video. Patients have the ability to shut off the simulation any time, but with each viewing their anxiety decreases as they become desensitized to images and sounds that once triggered flashbacks or nightmares. Virtual-reality simulators—like this one for 9/11 survivors—are designed with the same technology as the latest computer games.

Psychologists in northwest Turkey treated patients who survived the 1999 earthquake with exposure therapy using an earthquake simulator. Patients are ushered into a small, prefabricated house built on top of a "shake table." A computer is programmed to create an earthquake simulation, but the participants in the house can control the speed and intensity of the tremors and stop the simulator at any time. Patients treated with the simulator improved twenty percent more than patients who used talk therapy alone.

## Eye Movement Desensitization and Reprocessing

Eye movement desensitization and reprocessing, or EMDR, was developed in the 1980s by Francine Shapiro, a psychologist in private practice. She discovered that her anxious thoughts disappeared when she went for a walk in the woods, and she attributed it to her rapid eye movements as she scanned her surroundings.

During an EMDR therapy session, patients are told to think of their anxiety-provoking memories: the moment they saw their attacker, or the sound of a bomb blast. As they recall this memory, patients watch or track the therapist's finger as the therapist moves it from left to right and back again. It is similar to the classic scene of a patient being hypnotized with a swinging pocket watch. But during this procedure patients are told to replace the negative thoughts about the remembered events with positive ones. Besides finger movement some researchers alternately tap the left and right hands of the patient or alternate sounds in the patient's ears.

No one is sure why this technique works. It may be that the lateral eye motion back and forth stimulates both hemispheres of the brain, or it may be the exposure of repeated imagining of the real experience that brings about relief. Whatever the reason, in studies EMDR appears to help patients more than talk therapy alone.

## Stress Inoculation Training

Another avenue of therapy is training the patient to manage the anxiety that they encounter. Stress Inoculation Training or SIT teaches patients how to relax their muscles and control their breathing during times of stress. This helps diminish the symptoms of hypervigilance and the startle response. Practicing thought stopping or cognitive restructuring allows the patient to block those intrusive thoughts and nagging anxieties.

## The Effectiveness of CBT and Other Psychological Treatments

Cognitive Behavioral Therapy treatments for PTSD can last from three months to two years or more, depending on the severity of patients' symptoms and how much it adversely affects their work and social life. Long-term treatment might be required for patients who are suffering from additional problems, like depression, or alcohol or substance abuse. But the key to effective treatment is to begin shortly after the trauma. Researchers know that memories are flexible or modifiable for only a short period of time, usually a month or less. After that, the memory becomes part of the long-term storage in the cerebral cortex where it is more difficult to change.

Studies that measured the effectiveness of various cognitive-behavioral treatments found that on average 67 percent of patients were significantly better and no longer met the criteria of PTSD after therapy. EMDR had 65 percent show improvement, and exposure therapy resulted in a 70 percent success rate. This is compared to 16 percent for patients who did not receive any treatment at all.

## Treating PTSD with Medication

For many people therapy may be all they need to recover from the worst symptoms of PTSD, but some patients may need additional help through medication. A physician might prescribe medication when a patient is not eating or sleeping properly, or is struggling to get through the day. If patients are putting too much energy into balancing their lives with therapy, exercise, and stress relief, then medication is the next step.

Currently the Food and Drug Administration has approved only two medications for the treatment of PTSD; Sertraline (Zoloft) and Paroxetine (Paxil). They are both anti-depressant drugs called Selective Serotonin Reuptake Inhibitors or SSRIs. They work by blocking the site on neurons that remove serotonin from the synapses, a process called reuptake. This allows the body access to more serotonin. It has a calming effect on the body and relieves the PTSD symptoms of hypervigilance and intrusive thoughts, as well as countering depression and panic attacks.

In several studies SSRIs have been shown to actually reverse damage to the brain due to stress, by increasing the branching of neurons in the hippocampus. Neurologist, J. Douglas Bremner treated PTSD patients with SSRIs for a year and found "a 5% increase in hippocampal volume measured with MRI. We also found a 35% improvement in hippocampal-based memory function as measured with neuropsychological testing, for example the ability to remember a paragraph or a list of words."[25]

However, every drug has its side effects, and SSRIs may cause sleeplessness, nausea, anxiety, and restlessness in some patients.

Zoloft and Paxil are the only two drugs that are currently approved by the Food and Drug Administration for the treatment of PTSD.

Another class of antidepression drugs that are used for PTSD are called MAOIs (Monoamine Oxidase Inhibitors). They work to increase serotonin levels in the brain, but do it in a different manner. MAOIs block the MAO enzyme that normally breaks down serotonin. These drugs are not used as often as SSRIs because they interact with other drugs and with certain foods, potentially causing dangerously high blood pressure in some patients.

Physicians are continuously searching for alternative medications to help their patients and, although they are not approved to treat PTSD, many other drugs are used to treat similar conditions or specific symptoms. For example, patients who have trouble controlling angry outbursts may benefit from Clonidine. It is a beta-blocker, which means it blocks the rush of epinephrine that comes with a sudden outburst. The medication gives the mind a chance to evaluate the situation, like counting to ten before acting, to see if the situation really warrants anger and rage. Anti-anxiety drugs like Valium may improve mood and diminish intrusive thoughts and nightmares, and antipsychotic drugs like Clozapine calm violent rage.

# CHAPTER FIVE

# PTSD on the Frontline

**C**onditions in the military today are not the same as they were in World War II or even in Vietnam. Operation Iraqi Freedom launched in March 2003, presented soldiers with some unusual situations. For example, it was the first long-term war fought with an all-volunteer force in a combat zone that offered little or no relief from the constant stress of battle.

As of March 2007, more than 200,000 U.S. military personnel have been injured in the Middle East and treated by the Veterans Administration. Mental illness was the second most frequent diagnosis. Of the more than 73,000 Iraq and Afghan-

### Number of U.S. Veterans Being Treated For Post Traumatic Stress Disorder

| Period | Number of Veterans (Sept. 2005) |
|---|---|
| Pre-World War II | 0 |
| World War II | 25,278 |
| Korean War | 10,944 |
| Vietnam War | 179,173 |
| Gulf War (1991) | 19,356 |
| Peacetime | 9,087 |
| Total | 244,846 |

United States Department of Veteran Affairs Factsheet. Available online at: http://www1.va.gov/opa/fact/docs/ptsd.pdf

istan veterans, nearly 34,000 have been diagnosed with Post Traumatic Stress Disorder. To address this issue the Department of Defense developed new programs to deal with the mental health needs of soldiers before, during and after their tours of duty.

## Pre-deployment Training

Before being deployed overseas, troops are told about what they will see and do and how the stress of a soldier's life may affect them. One pamphlet given to new Marines acknowledges, "Overwhelming stress can cause an adverse reaction. This can temporarily interfere with a Marine's readiness. Most Marines are back to normal quickly, especially if they take action." Soldiers are encouraged to seek help immediately and to be aware of the signs of stress in others. It ends with these words. "Remember getting help is responsible—not weak."[26] And that is key, because according to psychiatrist, Andrew Pomerantz, "The stigma to receiving mental health services inside the military and out of the military is huge."[27]

A 2004 study found that nearly 80 percent of soldiers in Iraq and Afghanistan who had a serious mental health disorder acknowledged that they needed help, but only 40 percent were interested in receiving help and a mere 26 percent actually received care. Sixty-five percent of soldiers believed that they would be seen as weak if they sought mental health services and sixty-three percent thought their leaders might treat them differently.

This stigma over mental health can affect a soldier for life. According to the National Center for PTSD, there is evidence that, if veterans develop combat-related PTSD and their symptoms are untreated, the disorder will remain chronic for the rest of their lives and become increasingly resistant to treatment.

One of the primary goals of the armed forces is to educate all of their troops about stress, and to teach them that seeking help is not a sign of weakness. PTSD is an injury that needs to be treated just as much as a bullet wound. To make PTSD a more normal topic of conversation, the Department of Defense has encouraged high-ranking officials to talk honestly about their experiences and how war has affected them. Max Cleland, a former senator from Georgia and Vietnam veteran who lost three limbs in battle, has been candid about suffering from PTSD and has been affected by images of the Iraq war. "This war has triggered me, and it has triggered Vietnam veterans all over America." Through his therapy at Walter Reed Army Medical Center he says, "I realize my symptoms are avoidance, not wanting to connect with anything dealing with the war, tremendous sadness over the casualties that are taken, a real identification with that."

The strategy of being open and honest seems to be working. According to CPT Todd Yosic, a psychologist and commander of a stress-control team, "Approaching combat stress as a normal part of the combat experience has had a significant impact on eradicating a negative stigma toward combat stress control measures, enhancing our soldiers' willingness to seek help."[28]

## Life in the Combat Zone

No amount of training can fully prepare a new soldier for the real experience of combat in a foreign land. In Iraq or Afghanistan, for example, the frontline is not clearly defined. There are no safe zones. The threat is often invisible and unpredictable, and it surrounds soldiers on all sides twenty-four hours a day, seven days a week. It is difficult to identify the enemy. They do not dress in combat fatigues, but may appear as civilians driving a taxicab or walking down the street pulling a wagon. Every object is suspect: a baby carriage, a suitcase, or a lunch bag could be a potential bomb.

Not being able to tell the difference between civilians and enemy combatants is one of the most difficult situations a soldier faces. One scenario is so common that psychiatrists dubbed the familiar account the "bag lady story." A soldier is in the middle of a war zone or in a firefight and is approached by a woman wrapped in a veil and black gown carrying a sack. The soldier, being unsure if this is an enemy fighter in disguise and

A U.S. Marine passes some Iraqi civilians while on patrol in Fallujah. The most common situation that soldiers face in a combat zone is not knowing who is actually a civilian and who is an enemy combatant.

carrying a bomb, has no choice but to shoot. Afterward, the soldier might find explosives in the bag, or vegetables might tumble out.

Civilian casualties are especially difficult for a soldier to cope with. Children get caught in the crossfire and apartment buildings get bombed. These accidents are often difficult to reconcile. It is also troubling to see a buddy being blown up or have to carry a wounded soldier to safety. Soldiers often have feelings of guilt for surviving when others have not.

One of the most dangerous situations in Afghanistan and Iraq is being a transport driver. Convoys pulling fuel tanks are prime targets because they are extremely explosive. It is like sitting on a bomb; the soldiers never know when or if they will be ambushed, run over a landmine, encounter a suicide bomber, or be hit with rocket propelled grenades.

Soldiers have to protect themselves on the streets, and in their camps. Lt. Col. Bob Gerhardt, a frontline battalion surgeon, told CBS news that:

> You go out to a forward aid station, and you expect to get shot at.... But you get back and now you're back in camp, you take a shower, you'll sleep, go get a meal, and all of a sudden, 'Boom!' This comes out of nowhere and that's one of the things, I think, that has been perhaps the most stressful.[29]

Attacks on or near camp mean no restful nights for soldiers. They are constantly on edge, not knowing who will be hit next. One soldier recalled that the men he had eaten dinner with one night were all dead the next afternoon.

## Therapy in the Field

To keep soldiers combat-ready, the Department of Defense developed several new programs. "Never before in the history of warfare has there been such a coordinated detailed effort at mitigating the effects of warfare on service members,"[30] said Major Geoffrey Grammer, an Army psychiatrist. He is a mem-

Soldiers showing signs of stress in the field may be given a break, but are usually returned to duty within forty-eight hours. Data has shown that soldiers who go back into the field actually do better coping with stress than those who do not return to duty.

ber of one of many Combat Stress Control Teams that travel throughout the combat zone to identify soldiers with problems and help manage the stress.

"Soldiers suffering from combat stress do better if they are treated early, efficiently, and as close to the battlefield as possible,"[31] said Col. Charles Hoge, chief of the department of psychiatry and behavioral sciences at Walter Reed Army Institute of Research. The two hundred therapists, psychiatrists, and other mental health workers in the war zone set up camp and listen to the soldiers, encouraging them to talk about their experiences. They show them different ways to constructively reduce stress and deal with anger. They even administer medication if needed.

If a soldier or unit shows signs of stress, they may be given a break from their duties. For up to 48 hours, they get much needed rest, a shower, a hot meal to eat, and a chance to talk one on one with a counselor. According to the military, after a few days of rest more than 95 percent of the soldiers are sent back to combat. Major Grammer believes that, "Data would show that when you don't send folks back to face their demons, to overcome this or master this, they tend to do worse in the long run. It's the folks who go back that actually do better."[32]

## OSCAR

The Marines' stress control unit is called OSCAR, which stands for Operational Stress Control And Readiness. The mental health professionals are not in roving units, but are embedded within the fighting units, working side by side with them in the field. While field surgeons have been commonplace for a long time, a "battalion shrink" has not. But they are more effective than roving medical stations, because the commanding officer and soldiers learn to trust the mental health worker and will be more likely to share their feelings with someone who has experienced the same situations they have.

This strong tie between the soldiers and the therapists helps maintain troop strength. A troop commander's main job is to keep his soldiers fighting. He cannot afford to lose a single

# Teletherapy

Not all military bases have access to a trained psychiatrist. In places like Fort McCoy, Wisconsin, veterans once had to travel 600 miles to Fort Knox for a psychiatric appointment, but now they can talk to specialist on staff at Walter Reed Hospital in Washington, D.C. any day of the week. Using a private conference room and a secured videoconference live feed, soldier and therapist can talk as candidly as if they were in the same room.

individual. In the past, commanders felt that the mental health workers took away their men when they identified a soldier in trouble. Today, therapists are considered "force multipliers" because they can identify a problem and help a soldier deal with it while still in the field. They keep the troops mentally prepared and able to fight, taking care of problems before they reach a crisis level. But it is a difficult balance sometimes maintaining the health of the individual soldier with the fighting ability of the unit. They must foster the idea of resilience and reinforce the soldier's inner strength.

While in the field, therapists look for signs that stress is getting difficult to handle. They may notice a soldier with increased anxiety, uncontrolled nervousness like a facial tick, shaking or pacing, or outbursts of anger. They keep an eye out for those who are suddenly withdrawn from the group, or who have eat-

A soldier hugging his father after returning from duty in Iraq. If a soldier has PTSD the symptoms often become more obvious within three to six months after he or she has returned home.

ing disorders, sleeping problems, or are unable to concentrate. When soldiers are in trouble the therapists remind them that their feelings are a normal reaction to an abnormal situation, and recommend meditation, anger management, music, prayer and deep breathing. "They will never be able to forget what they have gone through," said Commander Dennis Reeves, "but the emotional impact will be lessened to the point where they will be able to be normal again."[33]

## Going Home

Today's military is more aware of the troubles that face a soldier when they go home. A soldier who has gone through "Battlemind" training knows that "Battlemind is the Soldier's inner strength to face fear and adversity with courage."[34] These skills helped them survive battle but can cause a problem if they cannot adapt when they get home. In the booklet "Battlemind Training: Continuing the Transition Home," soldiers are reminded of behaviors they will have to change. For example, in combat, split-second decisions to use deadly force is a necessary skill to defeat an enemy. But at home there is no enemy. It is inappropriate to overreact to minor insults or snap at spouse or children. In the military, missions were only talked about on a need-to-know basis. At home, that circle of those who need-to-know includes family and friends.

Soon after they return home, soldiers are given a medical screening and are interviewed by a healthcare worker to assess their mental health. Oftentimes soldiers downplay their emotions and will need another evaluation later. The second evaluation occurs within three to six months, about the time when PTSD symptoms, if they exist, become more obvious.

Among the more noticeable symptoms to develop is hypervigilance. These veterans have been on high emotional alert everyday for a year or more. Their senses have been fine-tuned to notice the slightest disturbance, the softest sound. They do not feel safe at home. Andrew Pomerantz says, "That's one of the things we're seeing in people when they come back—a feeling of an absolute lack of safety wherever they are."[35] So they have to make an abrupt about face when they come home. They have to turn off their senses and restructure their thinking so that innocent people walking along the street are not viewed as potential enemies.

The ideal window for treatment is about thirty days. "If someone is back more than a month and still having trouble sleeping, having nightmares, easily startled, avoiding watching the news, staying away from anything that might remind him of the war or just re-experience it in any one of a number of ways, or still seems remarkably different and on edge and irritable

# A Woman's War

Trinette Johnson slowed to a stop in her Chrysler Concorde as the traffic outside of Washington D.C. thickened. A highway overpass loomed up ahead. Johnson felt a crushing sense of danger. "I was just losing it," she said and called her fiancé in hysterics. She parked the car and walked away until traffic started to move.

Johnson had been home more than two years from her tour in Iraq and she still could not get over her fear. In Iraq an overpass was a prime target for bombs and surprise attacks.

Johnson is one of more than 140,000 women who served in Iraq and Afghanistan and was exposed to the extreme stress of combat. How to help women returning home with PTSD poses a unique situation for the Veterans Administration.

Women are usually the emotional hub of a family and many female vets have children. Female veterans find it hard to come home and shift gears from soldier to mommy. Johnson, mother of four, admitted that when she had her first reunion with her 2-year-old, she felt overwhelmed and walked out. But with therapy and patience, she and her family hope to make a full recovery.

Quoted in Donna St. George, "Iraq Vet Home but Still Haunted,: Post-traumatic Stress Invades daily life years after return from front," Washington Post, August 20, 2006, www.msnbc.msn.com.

with a spouse, then it's probably time to get into treatment,"[36] said Pomerantz. Today, there are more services than ever.

The military offers more frequent mental assessments, free counseling, and inpatient and outpatient care. There are 160 specialized programs, 108 PTSD specialized outpatient clinics, seven outpatient programs especially for women, nine PSTSD day hospitals, and more than two hundred smaller local veterans centers where soldiers can take advantage of group therapy. Residential rehabilitation programs are designed for brief and long-term inpatient care, and also target underserved

More than 140,000 women have served in Iraq and Afghanistan since 2001. Helping these women deal with combat-related stress once they have returned home has posed a unique situation for the Veterans Administration.

A virtual reality computer simulation showing animated U.S. soldiers patrolling an area made to represent an Iraqi business district. Psychologists plan to use virtual reality technology to treat soldiers with PTSD.

populations like the African American community, Hispanics and Native Americans.

## Virtual War

At more than fifteen Army and Marine centers, vets can get high-tech virtual reality exposure therapy. This option is attractive to many of the young men and women coming home from the Middle East. Hunter Hoffman, a cognitive psychologist at the University of Washington, believes that because of the video game set-up there are less negative feelings associated with this therapy than with other, more traditional therapies. He helped design "Iraq World," a program used at the Veterans Administration Medical Center in Honolulu. Another system, "Virtual Iraq," created at the University of Southern California's Institute of Creative Technologies, used graphics from an X-Box video game called "Full Spectrum Warrior."

In both systems, patients put on headgear with goggles and headphones, and control the action with a video game controller. In one therapy session, the patient drives along in a Humvee dodging burning wreckage and watching out for sharpshooters along the tops of buildings. The makeshift Humvee seat vibrates as if bouncing along rutted dirt roads. Through the earphones the patient can hear the chatter on the Humvee's communication system, the motor revving, and rapid machinegun fire coming closer.

In "Virtual Iraq," patients also experience the smells of combat: diesel fuel, garbage, body odor, middle-eastern spices, burning rubber, cordite, smoke and gunpowder. The smell machine created by Environdine Studios emits one of the eight odors on cue. This addition will help many patients for whom smell is a common flashback trigger.

Although it looks like a game, this therapy is serious business. The patients are monitored for heart rate and respiration rate to make sure that their stress levels do not accelerate too rapidly. As patients maneuver through this virtual landscape, the therapist asks questions and encourages them to talk about what they feel and what they remember. At any time, with a tap on the touch-sensitive screen, the therapist can add or remove stimulus like the sound of gunfire or the sight of burning tanks, depending on the patients' reactions. Over time, the combat situations replayed on the screen intensify until the patients are able to go through the scenarios with little or no anxiety. In studies done with virtual reality exposure therapy, patients have reported a decrease in PTSD symptoms ranging from 15 to 60 percent.

# CHAPTER SIX

# The Future of PTSD

Since the turn of the twenty-first century, terrorists have attacked the World Trade Towers and the Pentagon, a deadly tsunami hit Southeast Asia, a devastating earthquake shook Pakistan, Hurricane Katrina flooded the Gulf Coast, and war was waged in Iraq. These are only some of the headlining tragedies, but everyday there are thousands of people being abused, raped, pulled from car crashes, and recovering from attempted murders. It paints a bleak picture, knowing that these events can have a profound, long-term, negative effect on the survivors and society, but scientists are optimistic.

Geneticists believe that soon they will understand the underlying genes that control the chemical reactions that occur with PTSD, and neurologists are confident that they can pinpoint the effects of trauma in the brain. Psychiatrists hope to develop a more definitive means to diagnose PTSD, and pharmacologists are researching new drugs that will be more effective at relieving symptoms.

## Brain Research

Scientists used to believe that the brain was like a computer—hardwired and fixed. Once a person reached adulthood, they did not grow any more new brain cells. But thanks to new brain research, neurologists now know that the brain is adaptable and changing. Adults can grow new neurons, and damage to the brain due to stress can be reversed.

These discoveries have been made because of new technology that lets researchers see the brain at work. Functional Magnetic Resonance Imaging (fMRIs) uses radio waves and a strong magnetic field to measure tiny changes that occur in active parts of the brain. It identifies which blood vessels are expanding, where extra oxygen is being delivered from the blood, and where chemical exchange is taking place—all signs that that particular area of the brain is at work.

A patient is placed on a table and slid into the MRI machine. The patient is given specific mental tasks to perform like solving a math problem in his or her head, thinking up a shopping list, or recalling a terrifying event as the machine clicks and whirs around the head. In this manner scientists can see the

A patient undergoing an MRI. Some scientists are using MRIs to study the functional difference between a brain suffering from PTSD and one that is not.

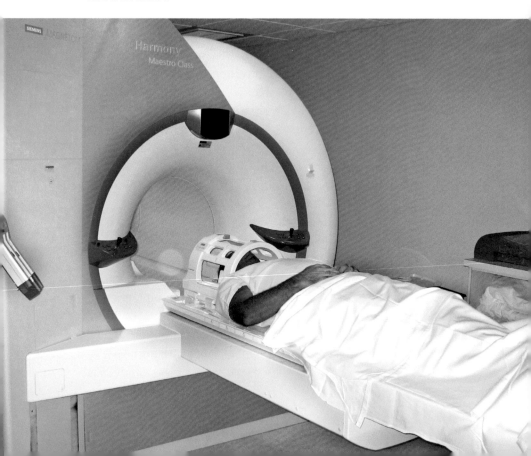

functional difference between a brain suffering from PTSD
and one that is not. The areas of particular interest are the
amygdala, the hippocampus, and cerebral cortex located in the
front of the brain. Patients who have PTSD do not show activity in a certain area of the cerebral cortex. This correlates with
not being able to turn on the part of the brain that controls and
balances the amygdala, the part of the brain that deals with
memory and helps control emotions.

Brain imaging can also reveal the link between trauma and
memories. A brain scan study took fMRI images of people
who had experienced 9/11 first hand and those who were two
miles or more away. The brain scans were taken while the participants recalled the event. A significantly different pattern
emerged between the two groups. In the close proximity group,
there was greater activity in the amygdala and less in the hippocampus, the part of the brain that usually restrains the
amygdala. Their memories were stronger because the amygdala kicked into high gear as the tragedy unfolded. The hippocampus's ability to evaluate and tone down the fright response
was impaired. "Individuals that were closest to the event had
multi-sensory stimulation. They experienced the event, they
could feel it, see it, smell it, hear it. That's another factor
involved in producing especially vivid memories,"[37] added Dr.
Grant Mitchell, director of psychiatry at Northern Westchester
Hospital Center.

Another study shows that PTSD alters the way the brain
perceives pain. U.N. peacekeeping veterans were asked to rate
the pain as their hands were exposed to a heat source. The
veterans who had been diagnosed with PTSD had more toler-
ance for pain and their brain scans showed less activity in the
amydgala.

In time, brain imaging may provide a way to diagnose
psychological disorders by looking at the brain pattern
revealed on an fMRI. Dr. Charles Marmar of the PTSD facil-
ity for the San Francisco Office of Veterans Affairs appeared
in front of the House Defense Appropriations subcommittee in
January 2007 and told them, "We're looking for an objective,

independent, biological marker."[38] Using fMRIs to look for the biological markers or specific patterns that occur only during PTSD would be a visible means of diagnosing a patient. Finding that physical test could change the stigma of mental health problems in the military. For the first time, invisible processes like making a memory, feeling fear, or hallucinating can be seen as clearly as a fractured bone on an X-ray. And knowing what circuits or neurotransmitters are involved in these processes will pave the way for pharmaceutical companies to develop better drugs that can target these areas.

## New Drugs

Although certain drugs, especially antidepressants like Setraline and Paroxetine, have been widely prescribed to treat

An Iraqi War veteran looks over his medication prescribed to treat his PTSD. Scientists are just beginning to understand why medications, like antidepressants, are effective in treating PTSD.

PTSD, scientists are just beginning to understand why they are effective, what they do in the brain, and what effect they have over a long period of time. They have learned that antidepressants:

> can block the adverse actions that are caused by stress, such as reductions in neurotrophic factors and atrophy of neurons in the hippocampus. More recently, we found that antidepressants can actually increase the number of new neurons in the brain.[39]

Pharmaceutical companies are continuously testing other medications that are FDA-approved for other disorders to see if they would be appropriate to relieve PTSD symptoms. One such medication is Risperidone, an antipsychotic medication, and another is a heart drug called propranolol.

## Fading Memories

Propranolol is a blood pressure medication doctors have been prescribing to heart patients for more than twenty-five years. It is also a controversial prospective PTSD treatment. Research has shown that propranolol may tone down the harmful memories that a PTSD patient experiences.

The theory is that the adrenaline rush that comes with a terrifying moment galvanizes the memory, solidifying it into the mind. When PTSD patients can't stop recalling an event it is because of this intense deeply ingrained memory. So if a large amount of adrenaline makes a person remember, then a decrease in adrenaline might make them forget. Propranolol has been found to reduce the rush of chemicals that sets memories in concrete, in vivid detail. It makes them more abstract and less painful.

In his lab in Harvard University, psychiatrist Dr. Roger Pitman attaches electrodes to a patient's chest to monitor heart rate, sticks a sensor on the patient's forehead to scan for tension and affixes another sensor in the palm of the hand to measure how much the person sweats. Through headphones the patient is

# Brain Washing?

It seems reasonable to want to help a child who witnessed a murder with a chance to lessen the pain of that memory. But many people are concerned with the ethical use of propranolol and wonder about the potential abuse of such a drug.

They argue that people's memories make them who they are. A drug that alters the emotional impact of a memory also alters the person's personality. It warps a person's understanding of his or her past. In 2003, the President's Council on Bioethics stated:

By 'rewriting' memories pharmacologically we might succeed in easing real suffering at the risk of falsifying our perception of the world and undermining our true identity.

Even though propranolol is not yet approved for PTSD, concerns will have to be addressed, concerns such as whether the drug changes a person's character; or if propranolol could be abused and given to soldiers who could then kill with little or no remorse. The drug also raises legal issues. If a rape victim takes propranolol to lessen the anxiety of reliving the event, will she still be a valid witness in a trial? Or would the defense use it as a way to discredit her testimony?

wearing, Pitman narrates the most horrible day of the patient's life; in the case of one of his forty-one test patients, it was the day he was almost stabbed to death. For others it was reliving a car crash or a factory accident. As each patient listens to his or her own personal gruesome details, the monitors record how anxious the patient is. The heart rate speeds up, the blood pressure rises, and palms become clammy.

But for some patients who were given propranolol in the emergency room just after the tragedy, and for ten days after that, the monitors remain fairly quiet. Reliving the horrible details is not so painful. Propranolol is a beta-blocker. It blocks the stress hormones from acting on the amygdala so that the event becomes just a regular memory, not one that causes a panic attack. Pitman's study showed that if propranolol was given within six hours of a traumatic event, a patient was less likely to feel symptoms of PTSD. Propranolol will not eliminate the memory, but as Pitman says, "It can take out the sting."[40] However, in order for the medication to work, victims must receive it soon after the tragedy occurs. The drug must reach the amygdala before the memory is consolidated.

Karim Nader, of McGill University discovered that in rats, memories are not permanently stored away as once thought. He found that when memories are recalled, they are transferred temporarily to short-term storage. Here they may be "edited" or changed more easily. Knowing that a memory is pulled out of storage each time it is recalled has prompted other researchers to see if propranolol works for older memories too.

A colleague of Nader at McGill, clinical psychologist Alain Brunet performs a similar test as Pitman. She presses her patients to remember over and over again a rape or a day of combat. When the patient is distressed, noted by increased blood pressure, crying, sweating, Brunet injects them with propranolol. Burnet hopes that propranolol will lessen the patient's stress response that is churned up each time the event is remembered so that eventually the "new memory" that will be stored is less traumatic the next time it is recalled. In 2006, twenty patients were treated with promising results.

## Genetic Research

One way to develop new drugs is to identify the genes that play a part in PTSD. In the past, genetic research focused on inherited factors that may make a person more likely than others to be negatively affected by trauma. Now geneticists are looking for the genes that control the creation of the chemicals that may cause the adverse reactions. The study of how genes can be turned on and off through environmental interactions is called epigenetics. Scientists believe that there is no one PTSD gene, but many genes that contribute to the disorder. For example,

Ultraviolet analysis of DNA. Scientists are studying the genes that play a part in PTSD as one way to develop new drugs to treat the disorder.

# Brain Bank

To study diseases like cancer, scientists can take a biopsy of a diseased lung or liver and analyze the tissue to determine the extent of the disease. But they cannot take samples from a living brain. Other than imaging the brain of living patients using MRIs or CAT scans, scientists must examine the brains of those who have died to learn more about the how the brain works. Researchers get brain tissue from brain banks like the Harvard Brain Tissue Resource Center in Belmont, Massachusetts. There they have more than 6,000 samples. There are brain banks specifically devoted to the study of schizophrenia and depression, and now scientists like John Krystal of the National Center for PTSD in West Haven, Connecticut, wants to create a PTSD brain bank.

they have found a gene that controls the level of serotonin, the neurotransmitter in the brain that influences mood and may fuel the fear response. Once they can identify the gene, the next step is finding out what environmental interactions turn it on and off.

Genetic advances are first studied in mice because humans share more than 90 percent of their genes with mice. Gleb Shumystsky, at Rutgers University in New Jersey, discovered a neurotransmitter called stathmin and its corresponding gene to be related to the fear response in mice. Mice without the ability to make stathmin (because they lacked the gene) appeared to be PTSD-resistant. After being exposed to a fearful experience, the mice showed less anxiety. They also had fewer connecting synapses than normal mice, which indicated that stathmin was somehow at work in memory formation. Memories are formed by making new connections, and without the stathmin gene they had weaker memories of fearful experiences.

Another chemical found in mice, gastrin-releasing peptide

(GRP) is released during an emotional event to control the fear response. In mice, a lack of GRP increases the fear response, creating more lasting memories. By understanding what each of these chemicals does in the brain and which genes control them, researchers may find new effective medications. For example, a drug that shuts down the stathmin gene might someday help patients with flashbacks and nightmares.

Hermona Soreq, a neurobiologist in Israel, has developed a drug called Monarsen that targets the gene that makes one of the chemicals found in large amounts in patients with PTSD. The chemical is a buffering compound that helps break down stress hormones and brings the body back to a relaxed state after a fight or flight response. But in cases of PTSD, the buffering compound continues to break down stress hormones and creates another kind of imbalance that leads to depression and anxiety.

Monarsen works by invading each cell that manufactures the buffering compound. It inserts snippets of DNA that adhere to the cells' DNA and prevent it from producing the compound. The brain's chemical balance is allowed to stabilize naturally, and the symptoms diminish.

## Promise for the Future

A new drug takes up to ten years to develop, test, and gain FDA approval, so patients might have to wait before they can be prescribed propranolol or Monarsen. While the world waits for a more effective medicine, the National Center for PTSD has promised to increase the availability of effective treatments like cognitive-behavioral therapy and train more therapists so that all people who suffer from PTSD can live a normal life.

Although more soldiers and civilians may develop PTSD symptoms, Ronald Duman, at the Clinical Neurosciences Division of the National Center for PTSD has hope that new research will lead to new treatments and perhaps a cure. "There's enormous potential for the future to be able to go into the brain and fix things. That is certainly the goal—just figuring out how to do it is the question."[41]

# Notes

## Chapter 1: Wounds of War

1. Charles S. Myers, *Shell Shock in France, 1914-1918.* Cambridge: The University Press, 1940, p. 25-26.
2. R.G. Rows, "Mental Conditions Following Strain and Nerve Shock," *British Medical Journal*, vol. I, 1916, p. 441.
3. Millais Culpin, *Recent Advances in the Study of the Psychoneuroses*, London: J.A. Churchill, 1931, p. 28.
4. Quoted in PBS, "The Soldier's Heart," *Frontline*, originally aired March 1, 2005.
5. Quoted in "Treating Men in the Aftermath of War: Post-traumatic Stress Disorder," *Connections*, Newsletter of the University Specialty Clinics of University of South Carolina School of Medicine, October 2006, p.1
6. Quoted in NPR, "Profile: History of the creation of the concept of post-traumatic stress disorder," *All Things Considered*, originally aired August 19, 2003.
7. Quoted in Jeffrey Gettleman, "The Stress of Guarding the Couch," *New York Times*, January 15, 2006.
8. Quoted in Beth Reece, "Invisible Wounds," *Soldiers Magazine*, May 2005.

## Chapter 2: Everybody Gets Stressed

9. Quoted in Harvey Black, "Amygdala's Inner Workings: Researchers gain new insights into this structure's emotional connections," *The Scientist*, vol. 15, October 1, 2001, p. 20.
10. J. Douglas Bremner, *Does Stress Damage the Brain? Understanding Trauma-related Disorders from a Mind-Body Perspective*, New York: W.W. Norton & Company, 2002, p. 116.

11. Quoted in "Neuroscientists Identify How Trauma Triggers Long-lasting Memories in the Brain," *Science Daily*, August 18, 2005. www.sciencedaily.com.

## Chapter 3: Society Under Stress

12. Chris R. Brewin, *Posttraumatic Stress Disorder: Malady or Myth?* New Haven, Connecticut: Yale University Press, 2003, p. 60.
13. *Diagnostic and Statistical Manual of Mental Disorders IV* TR (text revision) Washington D.C.: American Psychiatric Association, 2000, p. 463.
14. Quoted in Belleruth Naparstek, *Invisible Heroes: Survivors of Trauma and How They Heal*, New York: Bantam Dell, 2004, p. 128.
15. Quoted in Patricia Donovan, "UB Researchers Use Virtual Reality to Treat Car-accident Survivors suffering from Posttraumatic Stress," *UB Reporter*, Vol. 35, No. 13. November 20, 2003. www.buffalo.edu.
16. Quoted in Susan Saulny, "A Legacy of the Storm: Depression and Suicide," *The New York Times*, June 21, 2006.
17. Quoted in "Post-Disaster Response: Learning from Research (Part 2)," *SAMHSA News*, Vol. 14, No. 4. July/August 2006,  www.samhsa.gov.
18. NCPTSD, "What is Posttraumatic Stress Disorder (PTSD)?" *PTSD Fact Sheet*, www.ncptsd.va.gov.
19. Quoted in Michael Rosenwald, "The Iraq Defense," *Esquire*, Vol. 146, issue 4, October 2006, p. 74.

## Chapter 4: Treating PTSD

20. Quoted in Mazumdar, Sudip, et al, "Living With Fear," *Newsweek*, Vol. 145, issue 3, January 17, 2005, p. 27.
21. Quoted in Chrissy Casilio, "Help Through Research and Therapy," *Spectrum*, February 28, 2007, http://Spectrum.buffalo.edu.
22. Quoted in Naparastek, *Invisible Heroes*, p. 13.
23. Quoted in Naparastek, *Invisible Heroes*, p. 149.
24. Quoted in Naparastek, *Invisible Heroes*, p. 150.
25. Bremner, *Does Stress Damage the Brain?* p. 253.

## Chapter 5: PTSD on the Frontline

26. "Combat/Operational Stress: Information for Marines," pamphlet, U.S. Marine Corp, 2005.
27. Quoted in PBS, "The Soldier's Heart."
28. Quoted in Reece, *Invisible Wounds*.
29. Quoted in "Brain Rangers Fight Iraq Stress," CBS News, February, 27, 2005, www.cbsnews.com.
30. Quoted in "Brain Rangers Fight Iraq Stress."
31. Quoted in Betsy Streisand, "Treating War's Toll on the Mind," *U.S. News & World Report*, Vol. 141 issue 13, October 9, 2006, p. 55-62.
32. Quoted in "Brain Rangers Fight Iraq Stress."
33. Quoted in PBS, "Soldier's Heart."
34. "PDHRA Battlemind Training: Continuing the Transition Home," Walter Reed Army Institute of research, U.S. Army Medical Research and Material Command, March 8, 2006, www.battlemind.org.
35. Quoted in Streisand, "Treating War's Toll on the Mind."
36. Quoted in PBS, "Soldier's Heart."

## Chapter 6: The Future of PTSD

37. Quoted in " 9/11 Study Offers Insight into How Memories Are Formed: The brain's fear center created stronger memories for those nearest Ground Zero," *Health Day News*, December 18, 2006, www.nlm.nih.gov.
38. Quoted in Kelly Kennedy, "Brain Scan Could be Better Test for PTSD," *Marine Corps Times*, January, 23, 2007, www.marinecorpstimes.com
39. Quoted in Bailey, "PTSD and the Brain."
40. Quoted in Catherine Dupree, "Cushioning Hard Memories," *Right Now: The Expanding Harvard Universe*, July-August 2004, p. 9.
41. Quoted in Bailey, "PTSD and the Brain."

# Glossary

**amygdala:** One of two almond-shaped structures in the brain that deal with memory and emotion.

**cognitive-behavioral therapy:** A form of mental health treatment that focuses on how a person thinks and feels about something and changing harmful beliefs and thought patterns into positive ones.

**consolidation:** The process by which a memory is stored for the long-term.

**exposure therapy:** A form of treatment that desensitizes a person to a stress by constantly exposing them to that stress.

**fight-or-flight response:** The natural survival mechanism that the body has for dealing with the threat of danger.

**flashback:** A particularly vivid memory that feels so real the person sees, smells and hears the very sensations they originally experienced. The person is often out of touch with reality during the experience.

**genes:** Inherited material that controls a specific trait like blue eyes or brown hair.

**hippocampus:** A sausage-shaped organ in the brain that retrieves and organizes memories.

**hormones:** Chemical messengers that are released by glands and travel throughout the body.

**hypervigilance:** The feeling of being on constant alert, watching for danger and feeling on edge.

**neurologist:** A scientist who studies the brain and the nervous system.

**neurotransmitter:** A chemical that is released by neurons in the brain as a means of cellular communication.

**SSRIs:** Selective Serotonin Reuptake Inhibitors; a class of drugs that work to increase the level of serotonin in the brain.

**trauma:** An event or incident that causes severe mental or physical injury.

# Organizations to Contact

## National Center for Post Traumatic Stress Disorder

NCPTSD is the leading authority for research and treatment of PTSD. Their website is packed with easy-to-read fact sheets and more scholarly articles.

PTSD Information Line - (802) 296-6300
Email - ncptsd@ncptsd.va.gov.
Address: National Center for PTSD
VA Medical Center (116D)
215 North Main St
White River Junction, VT 05009

## National Center for Victims of Crime

The NCVC keeps statistics about violent crime and provides information for research and for those who need treatment.

phone—1-202-467-8701
Website—www.ncvc.org
Address: National Center for Victims of Crime
2000 M Street NW, Suite 480
Washington, D.C. 20036

## National Institute of Mental Health

NIMH provides information on all mental health issues and lists the most current research projects that are going on.

Toll free phone number 1-866-615-6464
Email - nimhinfo@nih.gov
Address: NIMH, Public Information and Communications Branch,
6001 Executive Boulevard, Room 8184, MSC, 9663,
Bethesda, MD 20892-9663

# For Further Reading

## Books

Penny Coleman, Flashback: *Posttraumatic Stress Disorder, Suicide and the Lessons of War*. Boston: Beacon Press, 2006. This book was written by the wife of a soldier who suffered from PTSD and committed suicide. She shares her story and those of others, and provides a history of combat-related PTSD.

Gary Paulsen, *Soldier's Heart*. New York: Delacort, 1998. Although this is a fictional novel, it gives a good account of the emotional impact of the Civil War on a 15-year-old soldier.

Carolyn Simpson and Dwain Simpson, *Coping with Posttraumatic Stress Disorder: Dealing with Tragedy*. New York: Rosen Pub., 2002. This title discusses various traumas and ways to deal with the delayed reactions that can occur.

Sara VanDuyne, *Stress and Anxiety-related Disorders*. Berkeley Heights New Jersey: Enslow, 2003.VanDuyne describes PTSD as well as many mental health disorders, how they differ and how they are treated.

## Magazine Articles

Matt Bean, "When Memories are Scars," *Men's Health*, Vol. 21, issue 9, November 2006, p. 150. Bean explores the research with the controversial drugs propranolol and monarsen and how they may someday be used to treat patients with PTSD.

Dan Ephron and Sara Childress, "Forgotten Heroes," *Newsweek*, March 5, 2007, pp. 29–37.A compelling report on how the military is caring for soldiers returning from the Middle East. Contains lots of statistics as well as first-person accounts.

Claudia Kalb, et al, "The Cost of the Katrina Effect,"

*Newsweek*, Vol. 146, issue 24, December 12, 2005, pp. 66-70. A comprehensive report on the medical and mental health care in the Gulf region after Hurricane Katrina.

Michael D. Lemonick, and Dan Cray, "The Flavor of Memories," *Time*, Vol. 169, issue 5, January 29, 2007, p. 102-104. This article discusses new research about the formation of memories and how PTSD affects them.

## Web Sites

**How Stuff Works—How Fear Works** (http://people.howstuffworks.com). This website gives a clear and detailed description of how people sense and process fear. It describes parts of the brain and the fight-or-flight response.

**The National Center for Post Traumatic Stress Disorder** (www.ncptsd.va.gov). The NCPTSD has clear and simple fact sheets about the disorder and how it affects veterans as well as civilians. They also have a comprehensive archive of PTSD articles and research being conducted all around the world.

**The National Institute of Mental Health** (www.nimh.nih.gov). They provide a summary of all the NIMH research going on as well as a PTSD fact sheet with up-to-date information.

**The National Institute of Neurological Disorders and Stroke** (http://www.ninds.nih.gov). As part of the National Institute of Health, the NINDS website has a section called Brain Basics. It describes neurons, neurotransmitters, and all of the parts of the brain and what they control.

**Your Amazing Brain** (www.youramazingbrain.org). This site has a section about stress and how it affects the body and the brain. It explains the fight-or-flight response and shows how stress can damage the brain using photos of real brain tissue.

# Index

# Picture Credits

# About the Author

Peggy Thomas is the author of more than 15 nonfiction and fiction books for children and young adults, as well as numerous magazine and newspaper articles. Several of her books have been placed on the New York Public Library's recommended list of Books for the Teen Age and listed as an NSTA-CBC Outstanding Science Trade Book for Children. She received her master's degree in anthropology from the State University of New York at Buffalo and lives in Middleport, New York, with her husband and two children.